IN DEVOTION & REBELLION

ISBN: 978-1-0369-6437-5
Cover design by EchoChamber Publishing
Printed in United Kingdom

For every little girl who was told to quieten down – may your voice rise louder than ever, and may the world finally listen.

WHAT IS A VOICE?

Your voice is not just sound. Not just speech. But that quiet, unshakable something in you that shares, not from shame or conformity but from soul. We often think of voice as something external, a way of expressing ourselves to the world.

But the more I've lived, the more I've come to believe that voice is actually something we're constantly discovering. Something we remember, more than invent. And if we're honest, most of us are sorting through a tangle of voices every day. Some of them are our own, many are not.

There's the voice in your head — the one that never really goes quiet. There's the voice that leaves your mouth — the one you show to others. And then there's the voice of everything outside of you — the world's expectations, judgments, stories.

There are over 8.2 billion people in the world right now. That's 8.2 billion physical voices.
This is before we even consider the call of animals, the sounds of modern machinery,

or the echoes of the weather and rumbles of earth herself. That is a lot of noise. And yet, the most powerful one of all of them is your own voice.

Even though our own voices might be the most important, what about the voices from the outside world? The voices of projection and expectation. The voices you don't see coming until it's too late, and you speak someone else's tongue. Or worse, the voice you think is your own, only to find you lost it years ago in the rubble of everyday life.

Our voices have been squashed and squeezed into various boxes from the moment we were born. They say we are born knowing how to cry; a full-bodied, unapologetic sound.
It is the first thing we do. The first proof we are here.

Over time we are taught to shrink our noise, to whisper instead of wail, until we learn that quiet means good and loud means trouble. We are judged by how we pronounce words,
and the volume with which we scream in pain and in joy.

Each year, our voices dim to fit the mold: speak when spoken to, don't be too loud, don't be too much. Before we know it, our wails become whispers.

Our voices are moulded by our history, by the land we grew up on, and the numerous opinions of others, until our truths must be edited for comfort.

Women's voices have been shamed and silenced to the point that we were burned at the stake or were locked up for quite literally having an opinion that wasn't delicate or to the tone of society. Men's voices have been moulded to avoid their emotions, shaped to perform strength while starving for softness.

We are all taught silence in subtle ways: a shush in the classroom, a sideways glance at the dinner table. And why? What is the reward of obedience over expression?

Piece by piece, we tuck our voices away behind politeness, behind fear, behind the need to belong. We trade our truths for approval, our questions for quiet, and our stories for silence. Until one day, we forget we ever had something to say.

I want to leave you with this early: You have a voice. Not just one, but layers of it. And it's okay if you've lost track of it. Most of us do. But a buried voice doesn't disappear. It waits — quiet, patient, aching to be remembered.

THE SOUNDTRACK OF LIFE SO FAR

To tell a story, you need one essential thing: a voice. Lord, did I have one of those growing up! However, many people forget that to be *genuinely* heard, we also need someone to listen. Sometimes, that's a therapist, a counsellor, a friend, a partner, your village or even your journal. Heck, I've been known to tell a story to trees at times just to get the swirling emotions and thoughts out of my body. I wanted to share them with no response needed.

When I first attempted to write this book, all I kept hearing was that old saying: "Don't tell tales." Add this to the memory of my dad telling me the stories of the boy who cried wolf and Rumplestiltskin as a child. And somehow, the idea of putting my words to a page became extinguished in this idea of telling the truth. Not that I tend to lie, but more that our memories and triggers can blur our truths upon reflection.

What I wasn't feeling comfortable about was that my truth, the way I saw and experienced the last thirty-odd years, would not be the same as others who had been there in the room or had experienced. All I can do is clarify here at the very beginning of our journey that these are my memories of how they felt then through my own eyes and how what I saw as a child might well be very different to how I see them as an adult today.

My ultimate fear in sharing it all — what would people think of me? Would they judge me for my failings? Would they think I was crazy for talking to spirits as if they were an extension of my own family? Top of the worry list: What if my ideas and opinions change underneath those worries? Something about ink on a page makes it feel very permanent. Because beliefs, like all other things, can change.

For the most part, my life can be split into two categories. I'm either in love with humanity – marvelling at its kindness, beauty, and brilliance; or want to watch it all burn to the ground in a gorgeous pile of smoking ash. I'm either all in, consumed by passion and purpose, or completely detached, wondering when everyone else will see how pointlessly exhausting it all is. There's rarely an in-between in my world. One moment, I see the world as a masterpiece; the next, as a wasteland that I quite simply do not want to be a part of.

This push and pull is exhausting, the constant pendulum swings between wanting to save the world and being the match that sparks the fire. And so, for years, I have tried to sit in a spot somewhere in the middle between creation and destruction. It's not always easy though because the place is, in my eyes, constantly moving. Sometimes the fire is precisely what is needed to illuminate the wasteland of today's world and other times, let's be clear here, I just need a minute to find a little more grace before I act.

However, to talk about it, to really go there, as if to take a torch and shine a light on the darkest corners of my inner caves? Well, the thought made me want to vomit, and I did. For quite some time the anxiety of this silent commitment to share took hold, until one night on my bathroom floor with my head in the bowl, I gave in.

A very calm and wise voice whispered into my ear that I should just write it anyway, and even as the acid in the bottom of my stomach tried to reach up and grab my throat at these words, I knew that voice was right. The first truth I had been trying to swallow for years was that every time I had written in my journal as a child or shared on social media as an adult, I was preparing to write this book, the one you hold in your very hands today.

I won't be the last woman to try to run from her story or lose her voice. I would love it if I were; however, when I look around the world right now, I can only hope that what feels a little too radical an idea for humanity today will soon become the norm. Until then it is my hope that by sharing my most brutal truths and a fair few epic failings, it may reilluminate a little of your own story. Perhaps you will be able to locate parts of yourself in my words and version of events and in turn that encourages you to not only share your own story but also to rewrite your future.

For as long as I can remember there have been more voices in my head than my own. Sometimes it's the voice of a parent. Sometimes it's the voice of a partner, a child, and often it is the voice of spirit. There are the voices that have quite literally saved my life, the voices that have kept me awake at night and the voices that lead me towards my future, however that looks.

It was Hemingway that said, "There is nothing noble in being superior to your fellow man; true nobility is being superior to your former self." I agree, and there are some things we need to talk about. Things that some might not want to hear, however, growth doesn't come from comfort. It comes from honesty, from facing what's difficult, and from being willing to challenge not just others, but ourselves.

So, let's embark on this journey of vulnerability together, through the words I wish I had said, more than a few that I wish I hadn't, and the many voices we encounter throughout life.

The world often sees stories as a ladder to climb out of our lives from. And for some part that is true, but for my part we can use stories to dig deeper into our life. Which is ironic considering my story starts at the foot of a giant wall.

Charlie x

We speak — not just to be heard, but to be known.

— Charlie Edwards, 2025

The Rebel's Prayer

O Wild and Unbroken, yet bleeding with light,
I lift my voice, not in quiet surrender.
But in the roar of a soul unchained.
I have walked the roads they warned me against,
Danced with the storms they swore would break me,
And still — here I stand.

I will not bow out of fear.
I will not kneel for control.
If I fall, let it be in pursuit of something vast,
Something worth the blood, the ache and the fire.

May I learn to wield my defiance with wisdom,
To love with the same ferocity as I fight.
Let my rebellion be not against my own shadows,
But against the cages that would keep us small.

And if ever I must bow,
Let it be only to my truth

To love or to something greater than myself —
Never in chains, but always in choice.

MAY 2024 -

Before writing this book, on a last-minute whim, I booked a few days of camping near Penzance's only available campsite. In true universal fashion, it unknowingly led me to a place surrounded by stone circles, ancient settlements and sacred sites. "Not your average restful trip," I declared, with a sigh to my husband as I looked over the map on the screen.

He didn't say it this time, but somehow I heard his reply, "It is never dull with you around, dear." Yet, a pre-book break before facing the blank pages of my laptop and sifting through my teenage journals still seemed like a rather good move. Let's be honest here, I think I was avoiding it a little. I might have agreed with spirit to write this book, but that didn't mean I was totally comfortable with the idea.

People take babymoons, I thought, so why not a few days of camping before birthing a book? If other people don't have bookmoons, I want to make it a thing! I quickly packed the essentials: a blanket, fluffy socks, tea bags, and a stack of books and headphones. Stories and music have not only given me the keys to unlock doors of remembering, but they have also, at the most challenging times, connected me to something much bigger than myself. I don't go anywhere without them.

I set up my tent and unrolled my sleeping bag a few days later. I spent the week with the sun on my face, listening to the wind howl across Cornwall. There is no other land I love as much as this place.

Each night, I dreamed of a giant wall stretching endlessly in both directions, as tall as it was wide. The first night, as most of us would, I passed it – searching for a doorway and trying to ignore the other women around me for fear of distraction.

Yet I couldn't help but see some kicking and screaming, others crying and hurling themselves against it. Meanwhile some simply sat with their backs to the wall, playing cards as if trying to forget their existence entirely. Older women lifted younger girls onto their shoulders as if creating a human ladder. I winced in fear that their crone-like shoulders may have been too brittle to carry more weight even as I marvelled at their determination to try.

On the fourth night, I gave in to figuring out the symbolism for myself and asked my guides what this wall was. They answered that it was a wall of many symbols, and this particular one was the wall of shame.

The words hit me like a blow to the chest, awakening something profound inside me that made me want to turn around and leave. I now understood why no one was looking me in the eye. I looked around at this endless wall, desperate for something to focus on other than the unsteady sway of my insides. And as I looked, I realised there were not thousands of women here; there were millions. Some trying to support each other in climbing over it, others digging beneath on a solo mission. I looked at the ground and realised this wall wasn't going anywhere. It was as ancient as it was new; its blocks were deeply rooted into the earth and reached as high as the clouds.

Then, something I had missed initially floated to the surface of my awareness. There was no sound. I leaned in; I could hear the birds, the breeze, and the wrestling of the trees, yet not a single woman was making a noise. Silently crying, silently digging, silently struggling, every single one.

A gasp for air was all I needed to wake myself in the tent's darkness. Grabbing my flip-flops and lamp, I walked across the dew-covered grass toward the toilet block. An owl's call greeted me as it returned to the field. The moon and I shared a moment with our feathered friend, and then I returned to my sleeping bag. I tossed and turned the rest of the night, yearning for just a few more hours of sleep.

The following day, I woke with a throat like razors. Never one to ignore the symbolism, I took myself off for a hot shower and had my coffee against the wall between the snapdragons. Someone once told me that in the Victorian era these flowers were a symbol of dangerous allure. I couldn't help but notice their tiny mouths stretching towards the sun. 'Dazzling but dangerous' I thought, I knew what it was like to have a voice and a mouth like that. At that very moment I knew what I had to do. I knew I needed to stop avoiding this book.

But more, I knew women's stories had not only been demonised but also weaponised. Why? Because they are one of the core threads that create freedom.

Stories are where the explorers play, and the dreamers go when the world becomes unbearable through its heaviness. And I wanted just a sliver of that freedom. I knew our voices were among our most powerful tools, especially as women. At one point, they were not only trusted and celebrated, they were honoured. In a different way that today we use words more often as weapons.

I felt a sharpness in my throat, like the last chunk of resistance within me rising to the surface. But spirit was showing me that to share my story and write this book, I too had to first tackle this wall of shame; not just mentally, but physically by putting pen to paper.

I closed my eyes and asked my guides to take me back to the wall. Without hesitation, I reached out and placed both hands on the stone that was mine. I wanted to feel this shame, I was so tired of fighting it and losing.

My hands began to vibrate as the stone in front of me started to tremble. I felt every moment that I had believed I was unworthy of love. Every day I thought I was flawed, every room where I felt I didn't belong, and every time I didn't believe I deserved all of the things.

The block of stone vibrated, then crumbled beneath my fingers, turning into sand and dust at my feet until I was left with a much smaller stone of my own. It merged into my hands and was gone. I felt no weight, only a rippling sensation through my body that settled into numbness, which, over the next few days, shifted into awareness.

Accepting my part in this wall allowed me to step through to the other side. In doing so, I was, in some small act, taking accountability for my past and future actions. However, I also realised that society had imposed much of this shame upon me. Once I recognised that, even more blocks began to fall away when I returned home. I was on what I called a pilgrimage of shame.

Dr Brené Brown says shame thrives in secrecy, silence, and judgment. My entire life, there was a silence I hadn't realised was there until now. The unspoken rules of every family or household, the questions we have that we know should never be asked. So much silence keeps us from another chance at freedom. For someone so often described as loud, I didn't fully believe I hadn't noticed before.

Could I unknowingly have lost fragments of my voice, and would they be returned to me? I knew I couldn't write this book entirely without using all of my voice and calling out some of the familiar inner voices we often experience. However, I still needed to begin and, in doing so, trust that missing fragments would return in the process.

Over the next few weeks, I saw myself on the other side of the wall as I began to replace my shame with empathy. Slowly, the writing started, and it began with the word of the first wall. Shame.

Shame keeps us up at night. Shame stops us from taking the next big leap. Shame is what this world uses to keep us caged, or for me, trap us behind a massive stone wall. Now that I'm on the other side, I think we should go back over it, at least for these few pages.

Let's return to my first memory of shame. Funnily enough, it wasn't bestowed upon me by a man like in many stories. This time, it came from a woman.

THE CHILD WHO NEVER WHISPERED

"Charlotte is not backwards in coming forward." – Perry Court Junior School Report. Aged 10

I'm not what I would consider an academic. When I say this, people scrunch their faces as if I have dishonoured or limited myself with my words. The truth is, I am comfortable with the awareness that standard subjects do not come quickly to me; maths, for me, might as well be a foreign language. As I have gotten older, I have increasingly realised I am creative. I adore music, telling stories, and entertaining; I love words. But as a child, I tried, oh, did I ever try! I sat through classes and tried my best not to chat or giggle. When I wasn't looking out of the window in a daydream, I did try.

In infant school, I would get into trouble for looking after the younger children of my class and not focusing on my work. I don't remember much past the milk cartons and my love for the library at that age, except for country dancing and the time I ran away from a teaching assistant across the school field simply because I loved that school field and wanted to chase the leafs on the wind. I had big ideas and big feelings I openly shared as a child. I'm sure the adults wished I had a zip across my mouth like that orange beloved character from the tv show *Rainbow* – "That's enough now Charlie, you have entertained us all for a short time with your stories and song, but hush now, back into your box."

Even when I moved to junior school, I loved nothing more than lunchtime on that large, expansive green space. Hiding under the swooping branches of the willow tree, making pretend campfires in the dirt, and telling stories to my friends that only I could see. When we weren't allowed the freedom of the field, I could be found swinging from the blue railings, singing at the top of my voice, and wishing for once they would let us explore the conservation garden as a sort of consolation for the fact I couldn't go and hide in the branches of my favourite tree.

Summer brought my favourite days when I would build a twig fire by my feet, curl up in the dust at the bottom of the willow tree and read my book until the bell rang. All morning, I would look through the window and crave the nest-like feeling of those branches. I might have been noisy, but it always amazed me how easily I seemed to slip through the cracks at lunchtime and drift off into my little world. Even as a child, my world was a land where nature was a part of me, dragons roamed, and a wolf slept at my feet every night.

Looking back at this memory, it seems such a strange thread to pull for a child who would have been described as "loud and confident", eating polos from Mrs Hall's burgundy quilted jacket and listening to her scold the boys for their rough play. Sometimes, I played with my classmates. I played alone when we had more space to roam beyond the concrete.

These memories didn't make sense to me at all until I realised I felt no shame back then. I never thought I wasn't thin enough, didn't know enough, wasn't wealthy enough. I suppose, at such a young age, I was luckier than many and I didn't understand shame at all. I now know that shame is often the key root of our resistance to sharing our stories, but for a child so confident and so open, how or when had I become reluctant to share my own voice and those stories in my head? What flicked the internal switch within me?

Secondary school felt like being thrown out of the fish tank and into a pond; it wasn't quite the ocean, but it seemed a lot more noisy and intimidating. Although, for once, I suppose I wasn't the loudest in every room.

Within the first three months, a teacher called Mr Evans bounced into my classroom with his brown curly hair and round glasses. His eyes danced with excitement as he peeped around the frame of my classroom door, declaring he needed "a quick word with Charlotte, Miss!"

I shuffled from my seat and quickly walked to the front of the room as fear tried to wrap around my ankles like weights. Had I broken some rules? I hadn't been here long enough for him to know my name, surely? If I had done something wrong, it was not on purpose, I reassured myself.

Dragging my concrete feet into the hallway, I prayed no one else walking past could see my shaking hands. Mr Evans closed the classroom door with a click and almost spun around on his heels in a dramatic scene opening. He said, "We are holding a performance, and I hear you are a bit of a singer."

My stomach settled immediately because I had been singing since I was two years old, in the back of my parents' car, to *The Only Way Is Up* by Yazz. I'd been in choirs and had already sang for everything from five people in a pub on a Sunday lunchtime to a couple of thousand at what was then the Colston Hall. A school production was a walk in the park; singing was my comfort zone. He explained they had a winter production coming up and wondered if I wanted to sing. The concert didn't include many from my year group as we were less than twelve weeks into term, but they could make allowances, he felt. I agreed, hoping it would get me out of double science with Miss Hulbert at least a couple of times before Christmas.

Weeks of rehearsals passed and I dived into the hall at every opportunity to learn about the lighting rigs, gobos and smoke machines. I'd sit with my glittery satchel on the scuffed black stage, my eleven-year-old legs hanging over the edge, bursting into song as sixth formers bustled about on lighting rigs, adjusting spotlights and changing filters. I wished my entire school day could be spent here, wrapped like the stage in these heavy red velvet curtains.

The night of the performance came, I sang *Fever* by Peggy Lee while sitting on top of a grand piano with lights dimmed low as if we were in a jazz club. My song was a total hit, so much so that many in the audience believed the song was a recording. Big celebrations were had in the car on the way home that night. As I snuggled under my duvet, I considered that maybe secondary school wasn't as scary as I originally thought.

The following day, I thought it would be as expected; after all, most of the year wasn't at the production, so hardly anyone would know about it. My first lesson was the dreaded French class. I knew the drill by now: you entered the room, and it was French only until you left. My teacher, whom we won't name for this story, ran through the registers of my classmates. "Bonjour Miss..." "Bonjour Stephan..." My turn oh, how I hated the pressure of the French register.

"Bonjour Charlotte," she paused. Looked up from her register. My gut twisted as I doubted that I had replied out loud. She smiled and praised me for my 'Magnifique' performance last night, then her face shifted as she looked back down at the register and added, "Although I'm not quite sure what your parents were thinking of letting you dress like that?!"

There were giggles, snorts of laughter and a couple of "oh burn," responses from my classmates. I simply froze, engulfed in the audacity of her words. I had never experienced this feeling before. This burning seemed to make me want to rip my skin off, stand on the rooftop of the highest building and scream. I later discovered the sensation was rage, which rippled across my body for the entire day of lessons and the forty-five-minute bus journey home.

As the day unravelled, I went through every emotion possible. Fear: had I done something wrong? The costume I was asked to provide was meant to be based on an old jazz club. I sat on a piano in a sparkling purple dress, black tights and lace-up ankle boots, with my hair slicked back in a low bun. I didn't think the dress mattered, but according to this much older and, as I thought, much wiser woman, it mattered deeply enough for her to bring it up in front of a class of 30.

Sitting in the luggage compartment of the school bus, I asked my friend if this was what women did, shame each other? This was not the Spice Girls' girl power I had grown up believing in. Was this a thing older women only did to young girls? Hadn't I done exactly what was asked of me? I followed stage directions; I hit all the right notes and marks. I felt embarrassed and ashamed in front of my classmates for something that I was proud of up until that moment.

Standing in the galley kitchen of Ashwicke, I explained to my mother exactly what was said. She was, of course, furious. I vaguely remember just wanting to forget all about it now. I took myself off for a shower to cool down, hoping to wash away the confusion. Then I curled up to journal before tea.

Journal —

I am so F'n Angry right now!!! (Yes, these are necessary, and here is why.)

Today, my teacher called me out in class for my performance. No, not my performance. Who does she think she is!? I bet she can't sing! So she thought she would judge me on my dress!!!! I'm referring to the purple glittery one with the split we got the other week at Tammy. So embarrassing. Everyone has been sniggering about it all day. As if secondary school wasn't awful already. I'm now the girl who was practically called a slut by her teacher!! She didn't look me in the eye when she said it either — coward! Just chop me up into small pieces and bury me somewhere quiet! Anything, but don't make me go back to school tomorrow.

Mum is going mental. She said she wants to go to school, but doubts if it will make any difference. It's too late now. She's already said it, and everyone knows! (How many !! There are never too many because this is a crisis, I Swear!!!!!)

Gotta go; the tea is ready!

I don't get it. I'm never going back to her classroom again. Speaking French is hard enough already. I hate her!!! HATE HER!

Cxx

P.S. Does it matter what you wear for a performance? Aren't you meant to stand out? Or is that wrong?

Clearly I loved an exclamation mark back then. If I didn't hate French lessons before that, I did after. From that day on, I redirected my attention to the flame that flickered beneath my ribcage. I switched off to French class and chose instead to tune into a tiny flicker of a flame that began to simmer just beneath the surface of my skin. Unseen by the world, once rage has been ignited within you it can feel impossible to use it in the right ways and for the right reasons to begin with, because you can't see clearly through all of its smoke. At that age, I didn't understand that rage can consume you, let alone that I had the choice of where to direct it. It was as if the flame led the way, and for a very long time, I was ok with it.

At the time, I suppose I felt I had two options: stop using my voice or use it constantly for every cause that was asked, and sometimes for those that didn't. Twelve-year-old Charlie took the latter option and took it to the extreme. Fire led the way, and I became the poster child for using her voice. You couldn't silence me; you wouldn't silence me.

I raised money for charities, appeared in the paper more times than I can remember, and even had a 30-second clip on TV for BBC Children in Need. I chose to use my voice for those who couldn't speak up for themselves and to call out anything I didn't like or agree with, whether you asked for it or not.

THE TIMES I DIDN'T KNOW I NEEDED ROOTS -

As school continued, so did the productions, performances, competitions, and travelling with other year groups, while on weekends I was running around backstage of the QEH Theatre like a kid in a candy shop. I was regularly singled out for my "talent."

Was singing natural for me? No. I practised. Long before iPads that clipped onto mic stands, I was 100% off-book for every song. From the moment I came home from school until dinner, I stood in the kitchen with the only cassette player in the house, singing repeatedly. I practised runs and ad-libs as if my life depended on it. I knew vocal cords were muscles that needed to be worked repeatedly to become stronger.

In those earlier years I would also attend a local youth club for kids who wanted to be in the 'entertainment business' where we would show the songs we had been practising and then receive feedback on them. Some were welcomed and others were a little beyond the way you should critique a child. We called one woman Mython the Python, and I would often find myself whispering to the gods for her to not be there certain weeks when I really wasn't in a performer headspace.

Not because what she was saying lacked truth, but I often think she forgot we were children, learning songs by heart between lessons and family commitments, and having the courage to simply show up each week and share at that age was huge. She would have been great as an X *Factor* judge, but perhaps not very inspiring as a mentor.

Quite quickly, I had regular venues booked most weeks and a large following. While most of my classmates were at home watching *Buffy the Vampire Slayer*, I performed two 45-minute slots with three encores, sometimes twice a week. And that was my solo starting point as a singer I suppose; between gigs and my weekly lesson with a singing teacher, you could say my world and my week were built around music.

Let's be clear here, no one could ever make me do something I didn't want to do or didn't believe I wanted to do. I always had a choice to stop, but why stop something that you love that feeds a flame inside of you?

I threw myself into the local entertainment industry so hard that by the time I was 14, I could control a room from my little stage with the ease and charm of an old timer on the circuit. It didn't matter if it was at the Black Cat in Bedminster or Cardiff Millennium Stadium, I knew what was needed and when. I could watch a new audience and sense when I was hitting the sweet spot or needed to step it up. The other side was that I could also sense a fight brewing minutes before any punches were thrown.

The one thing about being on stage is that it becomes automatic once you know the lyrics. Part of your brain becomes free between the melodies, and you get to people-watch from the stage or the corner of the pub. But people often forget that you can see them just as much as they can see you.

What people don't ever consider is this: before my step-dad moved in, the stage is where I first started reading people's energy and honing my intuition. I could tell who was on a first date, spot troublemakers as soon as they arrived, or identify the recently divorced woman out with her girlfriends to reclaim her freedom. I could see the colours change around people's energy as they listened to me sing a song they loved or a line that reminded them of a lost loved one. Like any decent DJ at a party, I could read the room through music and see it through energy.

As time went on I became too much for so many people unless I was on stage. I'm even aware that some of my mother's boyfriends didn't want to compete for attention with me. At the time, I wasn't consciously aware I was competing; I was just being myself, opening my mouth, and speaking without fear of the repercussions. As an adult, it's crystal clear to me now — the freedom and danger in this. I was in an adult environment, whilst most of my classmates were at home in bed.

This meant I was often mislabeled as "wise beyond my years." Was I wise? A little, but we'll talk about that later. It was more likely that I had taken on a role that I believed everyone wanted and loved - the applause that came with that role was a bonus.

But the downside was that I became the one pointing out the elephants in the room, dropping people into uncomfortable situations, and stirring the pot in ways many didn't know how to process from a teenager. I didn't realise at this young age was where life started and the stage ended, and I'm not sure many adults were around enough to notice this issue. Was I always in performance mode? Or was I simply being myself? I was vocal and possibly a little dangerous because it's all fun and games on a stage; the danger comes when you cannot tell the difference.

As I look at my children now at a similar age, I wince at the thought of them performing in social clubs and pubs. But I also think about what it must have felt like to my siblings to be the ones in the family who, at one point, everything didn't revolve around. And yet, we don't have the chance to see this when we are in the thick of it.

THE PRAISE THAT NEVER LANDED

My love of performing continued through secondary school; the flame grew, and I became more and more reckless. Not everyone had a problem with this; some people took my banter and humour exactly the way they intended. However, it was apparent to me by fifteen that we are okay with listening to a young woman's voice for entertainment, but when it's used to encourage change or point out issues, we vilify it. If I were on stage and sassy, I was praised. I wasn't as well received if I were in a classroom, playground, or coffee shop.

This could have been, of course, because I lacked patience with my timing, or maybe I hadn't met my people yet. For now, let's say a bit of both. Like most other secondary school students, I made friends, but these friendships followed a flash-in-the-pan pattern. We'd think each other was the best thing since sliced bread, then I'd become "too much". I'd say too much, let my mouth run away with me without much thought, and then it was over.

Usually, I was the devil people went on to talk about, and I moved tutors a lot of the time for speaking with little thought of the consequences. In my head, how I spoke on a weekend to an adult shouldn't be any different in groups of people my age. But I pushed through because no one would take my voice or shame me for using it.

It took me a few more years to understand that not everyone speaks fluent sarcasm, and many people didn't want the elephant in the room pointed out. I didn't just want to talk about it, I was likely to poke the elephant in the eye until it made so much noise that change happened. Many journal entries around this time are similar, but this one seems to sum it up:

Journal Entry —

They all hate me!!

I don't care, though; I'm not wrong. She said those things, I'm not lying. But now I'm the bad guy?! I don't think so, mate. I spent lunch in the library reading, trying to eat my apple quietly enough that the librarian didn't notice. Just me and the keeners. One day, I want a library, I think, but maybe not with the keeners, though. One on my own, haha.

Mum says she will call in the morning and see if she can get my tutors moved again. Amy and Studley said in maths, I could probably go with them in Mr Clay's class. Even Katie said I wasn't wrong and that some people just don't like being called out. I'd rather skip tutor each morning and go to class than keep moving groups. Not long left, I can do this. I can do this, right? I don't need or want friends! I am done.

*F*** I don't want to go back to tutor tomorrow. Maybe I'll just register, leave, and wait outside Mr Martin's office. The thought of walking in that classroom again makes me feel sick. The way they all looked at* *me today, the hate in their eyes. The thing is, it's the truth. I didn't lie. I guess the truth hurts.*

I should have told Mrs Mees about it while sharpening pencils instead of going to P.E. today. Not that she would have been able to do much, but still, she would have made me a cup of tea and given me a biscuit, I bet. Biscuits make everything better, well, that and really loud music.

Night. Love you Cxx

P.S. I lied; I do want friends. I might even need friends. Maybe I should have just shut my mouth and kept quiet.

I went from tutor group to tutor group. One minute with a large group of friends; the next, I overstepped the unspoken line and was banished. I don't think I was the only teenager who spoke before thinking. Don't most of us search for a way to have our opinions heard at that age? Each of us is in a rush to find our place and our voice, with little more thought than being heard. These days, teens use social media to voice their ideas, back then I had a microphone and an alcohol-induced public audience.

I'm not sure how much my opinions have changed over the years. I still identify patterns quickly, though now I hope to take a breath until I can share them more gracefully. But one thing remains: my intuition was and is never wrong. Back then it was my delivery that needed work.

In some ways I accepted that I was always the pantomime villain in someone's eyes and knew some people would always boo when my name was mentioned. But did it matter? When I considered what the majority of people were cheering for at my age, the booing didn't bother me as much; some days it even fueled me.

I moved class again, and built a friendship group again. And I honestly thought this time it would be different. Only it really wasn't. I then lost my best friend because a boy she liked said he liked us both. My response was something along the lines of: "Well, if you don't like one of us more than the other, I'm not interested," while she dated him. My frustration at that wasn't because she had a boyfriend and I didn't, it was that she couldn't see her worth. I received a lot of backlash for that. Again, it was probably my ungracious delivery. But how I wish at that time I had known that being labelled a bitch wasn't really a bad thing. What I really needed was a friend to process and talk my thoughts through without judgment. But we don't often find that at thirteen, do we?

In retrospect my voice was being judged from all directions from a young age. I was quick enough to handle a comeback on a Saturday night from a drunk in the pub, and yet the lines became blurry between the constructive criticism of singing teachers:"You need to pronounce your words more Charlotte"; mentors at rehearsals: "Your high notes are a little lacking, sing from your head not your belly there"; or the drive home from gigs in the back seat: "You need to say more between songs". I look at my youngest now, at that very same age I was and realise I was being constantly judged for my voice on and off the stage.

However at the time I was none the wiser and I simply kept moving forward. On the outside I wore my 'bitch' badge with pride because I also refused to feel ashamed about my feelings, thoughts or beliefs. I was talented, I was loud and proud. And the moment you think there is something wrong with saying that, you realise the world has been silencing women and young girls quietly through shame for centuries. I smashed down walls that other people saw as boundaries or rules. I was full of destruction like the Hulk, only no one seemed to know what lullaby to sing to calm me.

On the inside, I knew this badge kept me safe. It said: "Don't mess with me because I will tell everyone and feel no shame about sharing it." I managed to gather little groups across different lessons; people I didn't hang out with outside of the classroom, but for that particular subject or class, we were friends. For some people, my humour and loudness were totally fine. Possibly, they were the ones who had older siblings or were in adult conversations and environments at weekends, like I was. Was I always mature? Absolutely not, and for years those friendship mistakes kept me up at night until I realised I just had to let them go and remember I was doing the best I could with what I had and understood.

In my later years of secondary school, I remember sitting in history class with a knot the size of a tennis ball in my stomach. My body always responds immediately to things; I'll crinkle my nose or scrunch my lips. Possibly another thing that rubbed people up the wrong way, yet these were signs of "no" from my body. I loved History, but realised the records were written through a very particular lens. This particular lesson was no different.

My body was twisting on the inside as I resisted taking notes. When I had no choice, the margins were filled with extra questions written in my mermaid-tail purple pen to look up later. I remember a teacher once seeing my additional questions in the back of my book and commenting that I sounded pretty angry at religion. I was not angry, I replied (I probably was a little), I was just confused.

The next day was with my favourite History teacher. Trying to focus on her words, I wondered if she felt the same about history. Why did white men write all these records? Why was Henry VIII such a pig? And how did he get these women to marry him in the first place? Then kill them?

Where were the women's stories? Were they erased, hidden in caves or wells, or twisted to suit another narrative? I craved real stories and honest opinions. The recollections were written to scare people or translated by monks in a tower. I wondered why we only learned about kings around royal tables, fighting battles to inflate their egos.

Later in the term, I sat with my newly ordained teacher during Religious Education. I liked her for many reasons, although many of my classmates didn't. During our lessons, I began connecting the dots in my mind. The stories of gods, goddesses, and characters in the scriptures seemed to repeat themselves differently. It was as if I could see the web of them all being similar and connected. It's a religious melting pot in my mind. After class one day, I asked, "Aren't many of these stories very similar?"

Her face lit up, and she smiled, saying, "Of course. You see, we are all one, Charlotte. We are all one."

That flame grew even more significant as my voice grew louder.

I went to the place I believed every child should go when they have questions: the library. I loved my school library with its wrap-around balcony. Sometimes, I would simply sit there with my headphones on and my journal, writing about teenage drama and who was kissing whom under the bridge on a Friday night.

Yet the books in the library were an extension of the classroom. What I wouldn't give now to hand my younger self a Max Dashu or Seren and Azra Bertrand book. I often imagine what my younger self would have done if she could have heard Danielle Dulsky tell a story, or played with an oracle or tarot deck.

At 13, I needed to understand why my body felt that half of what my teacher said wasn't true or if they were true, they were missing giant chunks. So, I started reading autobiographies, and only by women.

I wasn't fussy about whose book I read. I would walk to my local Asda every few weeks to stock up on albums and books. I wasn't old enough to understand the difference between a well-written and a poorly-written book, but my love of books continued. Autobiographies were my passion for many years; through them, I made decisions about who I wanted to be and the types of paths I would do my best to avoid, until I realised authors often weave their secrets and the words they wish they could openly say in their fiction.

One day, I asked my teacher point-blank after class why everything she taught in History seemed one-sided. My teenage vocabulary probably didn't explain it well, but I hoped she understood. Sitting on the desk, her black boots sticking out from her long emerald skirt, she sighed and tucked a curl behind her ear. She was choosing her words carefully, and I could sense as much. Before I had a chance to doubt my courage and leave, she said, "I don't get to choose the curriculum, Charlotte, but I hope you continue to follow your curiosity. You are not wrong. The words of men are often the only ones we regularly choose to follow. They're not always wise or true, but we learn from our mistakes, as humans, not just men and women."

That familiar flame from year seven flickered brighter inside me. The following week I asked my other favourite teacher in the faculty the same question, and she said, "History, for me, is about asking questions, Charlie. When we get too afraid to ask questions, we stop learning." I carried her words with me right into the future.

I continued to do gigs on weekends, read books, listen to music constantly and try to make or keep friends in the playground. What none of those books or history lessons had done was help me with my lack of trust in men. And friendships, well, they appeared and disappeared over those school years.

I figured that the right people would find me friendship-wise, and a handful I still talk to now. For a lot of the time, my mouth and my opinions pushed people away. I do remember once though, being invited to watch the X *Factor* final at someone's house, only to find out halfway through the night I was the only one not invited to sleep over. I kept a smile on my face until internally I processed on the walk home that night and wondered if maybe I wasn't cut out to keep friends. Perhaps I needed to soften my words, wait a beat before speaking. Even now in my thirties, I look at my childhood friendships and wonder how I could have done better. And this is coming from someone whose school friend named her daughter after her.

All these years on I recognise that, for a long time a small part of me wished I could go back and do things better. Always a rebel, but in those teenage years, I wasn't aware of how devoted I was to making a difference in the world.

I was labelled a lesbian because I wasn't happy to be pushed around by boys and I was labelled a gossip and a bitch by girls because I said what I felt and saw. Was I misunderstood? Sometimes. And other times, I deserved it. But one thing I held onto was that I wasn't weak, defenceless or afraid of what people might think.

I was safe because my words protected me, and also those friends who knew me well enough knew they were safe with me also.

THE GOODBYE I DIDN'T SEE COMING

My dad left us when I was eleven, if my memory serves me correctly, just before I started secondary school or at least around this time. The circumstances, or events and behaviour that led to this aren't what's important here, but also even now in my thirties I'm not sure I even really know the truth of what happened. What's essential as we move forward is that we remember in my mind that back then I believed that he had cheated, left me and men cannot be trusted.

I remember so many things about my father; play fights in front of the fire, speeding over the flyover near Bristol city centre so fast that I thought surely the car tyres had left the ground, Saturday morning breakfasts at Tesco, accounts on Sundays, ending the week with his love for the *Antiques Roadshow*. I don't remember my parents arguing or having any heated discussions; I just remember the day he left and stretched his arm over the gate to pull the bolt lock across. Like that scene from the movie *Hope Floats*, it was only less dramatic on the outside because all of the crying and heartbreak was happening on the inside.

Until then, I had never realised parents could just call it quits and leave. I do however wish all parents had honest conversations with their children at the time of their marriage collapse, doing so might save a lot of therapy and late nights in the darkness of unanswered questions. As a child, I suppose it's not something you think about — a parent can just decide they've reached their limit, pack a bag, and never return except for weekends. Divorce is a clear reminder for me that you can be raised in the same house, by the same parents and have entirely different experiences and recollections. The same way I can be at a party with a friend and have a totally different memory of the night; we are all experiencing life through our own tinted glasses.

Unlike my siblings, I chose not to go with my father on weekends. Maybe it felt like a betrayal to my mother, maybe it was all the gigs I had in the diary, or teenage stubbornness? I do know that the last thing I would want is for the only remaining parent to leave as well.

Down to one remaining parent, I was driven to love, cherish, and perform for her. But also, I was never going to let a man or boy mistreat me or anyone I knew ever. The gigs went on for years, the PA being carried into pubs by my mother or my first boyfriend. It doesn't seem real now when I look back. But this period of my life taught me huge lessons.

Not only did it allow me to interact with adults at an early age in their environment. It also allowed me to watch. I observed social interactions from afar as I sang on stage or when I took a twenty minute break. I could see the friends that would later become lovers. Sometimes later was after a few pints, and other times later would be in a few months. I would feel a fight brewing in the energy of a room before it happened and I'd shoot the landlord a glance and then dart my eyes towards the possible trouble. He'd know what I meant.

I've been to gigs where people are trying to dance with the speaker stands while my friends are holding one and my grandad the other so they don't get knocked over. I remember it was so packed in one tiny pub with people dancing and singing that I had to stand on the green tiles in the fireplace with my back almost against the wall for the whole second set. We all took a huge deep sigh of relief when we were safe in the car after that one.

I've had gigs where the police have been called, lock-ins until the early hours, from social clubs, dingy pubs, swanky bars, prison staff parties, museums, charity auctions and Sergeants' Mess Balls across the country. By the time I was fifteen I'd pretty much seen it all.

Yet after every gig the conversation always remained the same. The 'constructive criticism car journey'. My mother would go through the things that worked, the things I could have said to the audience but I didn't. Then my grandad would pass over a bundle of notes from the front seat. This was for every time I smiled. Yep that's right, he paid me to remember to smile. Ten pounds a time. You see, I have a resting bitch face before it was even given that awful name.

Maybe I was overthinking the song I was singing, or what was coming next, what to say or whether I should change my set list order whilst people are up dancing. Or perhaps, perhaps I just have one of the faces that when it is in a natural position it looks like I'm in a mood. I can't really help it, that's just my face. But still my grandad paid me for a big cheesy grin, so I made sure I got at least two huge ones in at every gig.

I hated those car journeys with a passion, it was the quickest comedown from a good gig with a ton of cash in my back pocket. I would watch the rain slide down the window, hair full of smoke, the voices in my head reminding me I was 12 years old muffled. I had just sung twenty seven songs by heart and worked my butt off after a day of school. But I'd try. I'd try harder next time, because talent wasn't enough, you had to move, you had to smile, you had to own it. What could I have done better time after time I would ask, until I believed I was never going to be enough.

I grew up to see that my success was somehow an extension of my mother's and that she was doing the best that she knew how. But as I got older I moved from solo performing to being in a band. With this bunch of guys, the drive home wasn't constructive criticism, it was Tony Robbins in the van, wrapped up under a sheepskin jacket, or jazz music on low whilst we talked about life. Don't get me wrong, the boys were a total pain in the ass but I was very lucky to have them when I needed them most.

Each member of the band filled a space in my heart that I didn't understand at the time. I wasn't huge on boyfriends due to firstly always being busy on a weekend and secondly I had become fiercely independent, plus who has time for boyfriends when you are on the road. Being around these guys gave me exactly what I needed.

We had other members come and go, including a German drummer to begin with. My god how I dreaded the moment he would get his metronome out of his biscuit tin. Timing was never my best skill. In fact for several years I would need a nod from Pete the bass player on certain songs when I was coming in, because I would lose count watching someone in the crowd.

There are so many things I learnt from being in a band and singing on the circuit with a group of men. So many lessons I learned so early on about different audience energy. It actually fascinates me when I go out with other people and they don't notice or sense what is going on in the room around them.

I could be out with a friend and they would have no clue what was happening on the other side of the room. Yet I'm downing my drink because I know shortly it will kick off and we'll need to quickly leave. It wasn't a protective thing, not because I didn't feel safe. It's simply always been something I have done, even in primary school I was always aware of the difference of a classroom on a Monday morning compared to some Thursday afternoons.

All through secondary school, I had held this little part of me a secret. That wasn't out of shame or fear of misunderstanding, but because, in my head, I had already sorted it out. I locked it away and threw away the key because that's what the oldest daughters and big girls do. We can handle it; we are tough. I didn't keep much a secret back then, but this sense of energy and connection was for me only.

In school I would happily put a teenage boy in his place or tell him where to go, which led to an almost year-long rumour that I was a lesbian. I still find this hilarious. To clarify, I love men, and I also believe we fall in love with someone's soul, not the body they came to this planet with at this time. But as children, this could be the only reason, right? "She must hate boys and love girls. Why else would she tell me to stop twanging her bra strap, or she would break my fingers?"

I would happily put boys in their place when they stepped out of line, and if that meant threatening violence, then so be it. To this day, I have never been in a physical fight; I found my weapon of words early. I also had brief boyfriends at this point, inside and outside of school, but to the school rumour mill it didn't matter. If I'm honest it didn't matter to me either; it gave me an extra shield I was pretty happy to carry through life for a long time yet.

In my last term, I hit a boy for calling me a slut. Well, I didn't technically hit him; I grabbed hold of his head and smacked it against the school bus window not once but twice. It was over as quickly as it started because the bus had stopped and I was getting off. It's still as clear as day in my mind as I shoved my messenger bag back onto my shoulder and suggested he should choose his words more wisely. Then I got off the bus, walked down the road to my house, and thought very little of what had happened. My brother saw the incident and told my mother. She asked me if he deserved it. I said he did, and that was that.

I am not and never will be a violent person, nor would I encourage anyone else to be violent. It doesn't solve anything; in fact, it often makes things a heck of a lot worse. The following morning, I went to my tutor as usual, but after I registered, the tutor told me I needed to go and see my head of year. I looked at him in shock as he tried not to smirk a little. This had clearly been the talk of the staff room that morning. I asked if I should take my bag, and he said he felt I might be a while. So I trudged across the buildings to my head of year's office. Barely through the door, he said: "Charlie, I was surprised by what I heard this morning."

... Silence...

"Oh, why's that, sir?"

"Well, I had Larry's mother on the phone this morning..." I nodded slowly, knowing there was no need to fill the gaps.

"She says you are a danger to her son's safety..." It's too late. The smile is plastered on my face, and I can't pull it back inside.

He pauses. "I'm not so sure this is something to be proud of, young lady." I force my face to neutralise, and it ripples down my body to let out the slightest shrug. Damn it, he wasn't happy.

Perhaps it was knowing I was almost in my last term, or maybe that Larry had deserved it. All these books I had read, all these history lessons and stories and for once, I was a danger to someone's safety. A girl was a danger to a boy's safety. It felt powerful in a strange way that I didn't mind. It felt as if this was a small win for every time someone had pinched my butt in the corridor, or thought they had the right to comment on my body. This small act of defiance didn't seem to match the behaviour of the boys, yet here I was being dragged across the coals.

"Do you want to tell me what happened?" He asked.

"He called me a slut as I was walking past his seat, so I smacked his head against a window, sir."

He turned to his desk and sighed. "You are now banned from the bus for the remainder of the term."

"The thing is, sir, my mother will go ape at that; she can't drive me to school and get my brother and sister to their school on time."

Not wanting to deal with my mother again, he informed me he would tell Larry's mother that I would be sitting downstairs only on the bus and that if I even spoke to him again I would be suspended. As I let myself out of my head of years office and the door shut behind me, I muttered under my breath, "Just a few more weeks, Char... a few more weeks."

Boys hadn't always shown me bad examples, either. Sitting in Drama class later that month, surrounded by the same group of boys I always worked with, I wondered how girls and boys could be so different mentally. In Drama, we laughed and possibly had some adult banter that only Mr. Gallop could handle and sometimes joined in with. I didn't mind being one of the boys then.

Shout out to that group of lads. When you write these types of recounts, it can feel one-sided, and a bit like a 'poor me' story. There was a small group, or a couple to be fair, that were fun to be around and allowed me to be myself. Small and few, but often that's all you need to keep trying.

I remember around that time being warned by a singer named Kaz not to "ever go near the men's backstage room when a certain 'entertainer' is in there." This was my first example of a woman protecting a woman so vocally. As an intuitive kid, I knew immediately something terrible had happened to someone; later that night, as I watched her avoid the man in person, I hoped she wasn't talking from her own experience and instead was simply an older woman warning a young girl.

I also remember a boy in my Maths lesson saying something to me that I refuse to put on this page, for my teacher to overhear it, read him the riot act in front of the entire class and to check I felt safe to continue in his classroom. I often wish I could thank Mr Clements for that morning. In fact, for every handful of things that frustrated me with those school years, there is a teacher or person that I remember just being extra illuminating in a world I didn't understand.

I wasn't proud of many things in my school years, yet every time Larry's Mum met him at the bus stop for the next few weeks to make sure he got home safely, I will admit I felt just a little satisfaction that, for once in my life, a woman was on top. Writing this makes me wince as an adult, but that's a part of growing up: not seeing our growth and being okay with all its phases.

To finish my time at secondary school and fuel my internal fire, my English teacher assigned *The Handmaid's Tale* and *Of Mice and Men* for our GCSE studies. I thought I couldn't love her more after she gave us Baz Luhrmann's *Romeo and Juliet* the year before, but I was wrong. Being in her class encouraged me to explore fiction, unpick stories, and look for hidden messages and symbology that whispered between the lines.

It was in those classrooms and between those bookcases that I realised the history we study is simply a collection of stories written by those already influenced in hopes of shaping those that follow on in later years. I understood the purpose of it, the power of the memory, but what I couldn't see was how we change things for the future.

The last week of school, I returned my library books and emptied my locker. In the back, behind the knee-high blue stripe gym socks I hadn't worn since my first term, was a crumpled Post-it. I pulled it out, about to throw it into the rubbish bag, until I saw the word "Hunter" on the edge. Uncrumpled, it read: "Until the Lion learns to write, every story will glorify the hunter." I shoved the Post-it in my rucksack and also locked it in my heart.

As I prepared to leave school, with a new-found drive to rewrite history and a determination never to stop sharing my voice, I sat in the luggage compartment of the school bus for the last time, reading my leavers' book.

It was as if, all of a sudden, I realised, on one hand, the world might not be keen on a loud woman who defends others and themselves. Yet, on the other hand, every page of my book was filled with notes of thanks for the advice and lines sharing how they appreciated how I had helped someone through that hard time. If I am honest, I wasn't sure where this wisdom came from because, looking at the school as we pulled away for the final time, I could only see the bonfires I had created.

Shoving my leavers' book into my bag, I prayed that college would be different, right? It's the perfect time to recreate yourself, polish your act, and try again.

My voice is not too much. (repeat)

My truth is not too loud. (repeat)

My words are not weapons – they are remembrance. (repeat)

I belong to this sound. (repeat)

I trust what comes through me. (repeat)

THE INVISIBLE ROLE OF THE ELDEST

The voice of an oldest daughter is bold, it's often deeply in the masculine because she was unknowingly raised that way through various societal and family imprints. We see it in memes regularly nowadays or reels of attempted humour, but is it actually funny? I'm not sure what combination of imprinting mine was. But I do know that not having a father in the home played a key role in how safe I felt.

Not long after he left I woke in the middle of the night at the clang of our side gate. I realised at that very moment that this was why they probably had never put any oil on it – to alert them when someone came down the side of the house. Funny how younger Charlie hadn't considered this until that night.

The metal hit the side of the house and the sound echoed right up to the loft conversion where I slept. Leaping from my bed, I tiptoed to my mothers room to find her awake also. We switched on the landing light to find two men outside with their backs to the porch doors waiting. My stomach dropped at the realisation of how unprotected we were. One woman and four children in the house.

My mother rang the police I think, and I was shuffled back to bed. I think a hammer was found by the back door at the time, but I cannot be sure. The fact was, the noise of the gate had woken us and the lights had scared off the men. That's all my eleven year old brain needed to know.

Quite naturally I seemed to take on an adult role in our household – remember my school reports did warn of my mothering the younger children before this, so we must not place the blame on one situation or person. Sometimes the reasons stack up and often unknowingly. My misplaced sort-of-mother role to my siblings pushed them away, I fear.

Not only trying to manage my emotions but also the entire dynamics of the family. It placed me in a sort of 'best friend' role to my mother (not recommended) and distanced me from my siblings in many ways. But more importantly, it was another thing that catapulted me through childhood at an unnatural pace. As a child I suppose I tried to keep the peace in the home because in my mind, if everything was calm, I could feel safe.

So for me, college was yet again an escape. Like Hansel and Gretel, I followed the path towards anything that felt like freedom and nothing like responsibility. Admittedly no one had outright given me the responsibility of my siblings and the emotional consistency of the household, however a part of me took college as a pathway for myself.

THE ARCHITECTURE OF DEFENCE

By September, I had spent a summer working many campsites and competitions and was hopeful that college was going to give me the place I had been looking for. At this point I knew that off of the stage my energy was too big, loud, and shiny for most people. In college, I chose subjects of joy; I took Photography, Psychology, English Literature, Drama and Performing Arts. The way I saw it, I was already working two jobs at this point, and I still didn't know what I wanted to be or do, so I followed my curiosity in hopes it would lead me towards a more transparent idea; sort of career path before I needed to commit to university.

I immediately loved meeting a kaleidoscope of new people. The best part was that most of them didn't know me, and my days were filled with things I loved and found fascinating. College gave me a chance to witness other voices and sometimes see how limited my life experience had been up until this point. There were voices from all over the world and somehow college seemed to have a room or a table for them all. For the first time in my education I felt as if there was not only room for everyone, but enough space for us to all find our people without judgement.

It was inviting and exciting all at the same time. I spent my time between the Theatre Studies building and the dark room. One in the spotlight and the other nestled in the darkest corner, headphones on, developing photos through lunch break. You'd think I should have been born a Gemini.

I enjoyed my classes. Most of my teachers understood me on levels I had hoped for, and I realised that the chosen subjects told stories in different formats. I found a much-needed calm in the Photography darkroom that, to this day, I hope I will return to. College had this capacity of acceptance that the rest of the world forgets is possible.

Everyone had opinions, ideas, and different upbringings that opened my eyes to how much of the world there was to explore, yet everyone seemed to get on. My teachers had time to debate and explore topics more freely, and if I had a free period, I could take myself to the field with a book or to McDonald's with friends. It was as if everyone had more oxygen and space on campus to be more of themselves and for everyone to be heard. Those years taught me there was an entire world out there and there was space for us all.

College was also the place I was reminded I wasn't the best singer. This wasn't entirely new to me; I was constantly the one who was on call back, or who just missed the final three for a TV show. I definitely wasn't the most confident or most well-trained. But it was college that made me realise perhaps I was here to be or do something else with my life, maybe a different type of stage. I wasn't sure, but for two years I managed to float from social group to social group, not popular enough to sit on the left-hand side of the common room by the door, and definitely not in the booths with the rugby players and second years. But popular enough to flit in and out of most groups comfortably, never fully fitting in, and never fully standing out.

I made lifelong friends in college and re-found ones I had somehow lost from primary school. Friendships and memories I am still so grateful for today. Weekends and evenings spent in the Goff family kitchen or snuggled up in the Nicholas family's living room with a tummy full of roast dinner. Places outside of the stage that accepted my fierceness into their family when I'm not sure even I had fully accepted it myself.

During those years I got to witness many many examples of relationships. It must have been all the hormones and new people in one place. Large amounts of that first year were spent partnered off and focused on dating. It wasn't that I wasn't interested in dating, it was more that I was working two jobs, had multiple rehearsals and was usually behind on my actual college studies.

As I watched my friends couple up I slowly began to realise that over the past few years, my mother's negative beliefs and distrust of men had rubbed off onto me a little too much, leaving an intense wound that all men would let you down and eventually leave. With my few college boyfriends, this showed up quite clearly; I wasn't the princess in a tower waiting for someone to choose me; I was the dragon.

I believe it was a choice I made through strength and courage, but as the college years went on, I realised it was much more profound. But rather than do some wound exploration, — what teen wants to do that — In my free time, I took to the dance floor.

While my friends were dating or looking for relationships, I was dancing. God, I loved to dance; I often finished a gig and got dropped off in town to catch the last few hours of the nightclubs with friends. For me, nightclubs were for the music, to feel that bass thump through your body, and to soak up the atmosphere when everyone was connected to the same song. For a lot of them, it was to drink. Being in pubs and clubs at such a young age, I wasn't overly fussed about alcohol, and I most certainly knew what it could do to people. Unlike most, this wasn't my first time in a club or unsupervised in an adult environment.

I dated occasionally, but for someone who spent so much of her free time entertaining everyone, counting intros, and trying to work out harmonies, nightclubs were for me and the music, and the music saved me over and over again.

Reflecting on my few early relationships, I now see that the shards of my mother's broken heart that had been impaled into my skin were both a blessing and a curse. They taught me to know who I was getting into a car with at midnight for a lift home. My distrust saved me a lot of heartache and many of my girlfriends from dangerous times in the dark corners of nightclubs. But it also made it incredibly hard to get close to me. I've had drinks poured over me and been called "stuck-up" because I responded, "I'm good, thanks, I can buy my own drink."

To the outside world, I loved myself and thought I was too good for people, when the truth was incredibly different. I was so distrusting of the world that my quick wit and sarcasm had become a reinforced wall to protect me from the men who did terrible things and let you down, or left just when you trusted them.

My mother's fear and wounding around men also taught me that you should never let a man hurt you. I don't often have the grace to find things to thank my mother for, yet this spark of a belief that men should treat me well – though it was shared through her own mistakes and history of betrayal – is the single thing I am grateful she gave me.

But they also placed me in a spot of pretending; as if those pieces gave me a false sharpness that kept me pretending I was strong, independent, and brave; so fucking brave. As if my sharp words and quick wit would keep me safe.

College showed me that teenage love is intensely quick. It swallows you into a world of mixtapes and emotions you see in movies and read about in books. Perhaps it's because, as teenagers, we tie the idea of love to so many expectations and requirements that we are often sold around the word 'love' and what it means before we truly understand how to love ourselves.

Now, as an adult I see that as teens we already have a very fixed reference for what love is, how it feels and what it looks like — and yet we haven't quite figured out what our own version of love is like. Still focused on the examples we have seen at home or in the movies, many of us go through almost trial and error phases. And let's be clear there is a lot of fun to be had at that age.

After college I stopped performing almost all together unless I was in the shower or maybe karaoke with friends. If anyone asked I would tell them, “There are people who want it more than me”. Because that was the truth; no casting, role or TV slot was going to convince me to sell my soul or otherwise. Something in my heart wasn’t willing to sell my voice into a system that was designed to own an artist or, worse, make them compete rather than collaborate.

I dreamt that one day I’d do a theatre tour of some sort, where we would gather — tell stories, laugh and sing and connect in the way our voices were originally intended rather than the way the industry has currently ended up.

Over the years I found love for people in many different ways, but I’m not sure that during college I knew how to love myself, though from the outside most would have had no idea of the pain I was in. Since my dad had left I suppose my body was in a very performer/protector mode and I had no clue how or when it was safe to switch that off. Relationships required bravery and vulnerability. Neither, at that time, I was sure I was capable of.

Through those brief college years, I met some incredible people and some not-so-incredible ones. In the last year of college, I very briefly dated a guy. I loved his family and his friends as if they were my own and somehow, during the short time we were dating, I knew I would have ended up destroying him. No matter how hard he would have tried, he would have swaddled me to the point that I would have suffocated – or worse, I would have broken his heart to the point of no repair.

He adored me and I really didn't know how to handle it, or how to hold it for longer than a few weeks. I couldn't allow that to happen for either of us. So it ended as quickly as it started. That's the poetic way of putting it isn't it, or maybe I just got scared at the unfamiliar feeling of safety and ran back behind those very high walls I had built around myself.

At the time we were living with my stepdad and my mum had recently had another baby. My step-dad was a hardworking man, and very intense compared to the father I had grown up with. But he was also a bit of a drinker, and with his drinking came an unspoken timer in the back of my mind around when it was best to disappear. As I got older, it became easier to just stay out of the house as much as possible.

I think we so often discredit first loves or teenage dating as an influx of hormones and poor decisions. But those years gave me huge sign posts towards my greatest lessons. Being a fighter was easy, but learning to love? That was on an entirely new level of existence. I refused for a very long time to acknowledge it existed. I could give love, god I could share love! But love myself and see how loved I deserved to be? Not so easy.

Which is mad, right? I was talented, young, full of life and yet something in me believed I should always do better, be better. There was always room for improvement, because if I wasn't seen to be improving or trying to be better, then how could anyone ever love me, and if I wasn't the best at all times, then why would anyone ever stay?

Journal Entry —

Now what? Literally now what?! I have a summer full of gigs, but after that — nothing! Everyone else is going to uni, I think. I don't know exactly; no one is really talking about it, and I suppose I should have probably asked an adult. Am I an adult now? I don't feel like one, that's for sure. Who decides when we become adults? Old enough to make our own decisions? I don't think it is wise for that to be me at the moment.

I suppose if I don't know what I want to do for a career, and I don't really have any direction, I could just pick up some more hours on the shop floor and see what comes from there. Something is bound to come up, right?

Why does everyone else seem so excited? I just feel as if there was a map — something that was expected — and now there's nothing. No path. No map. I suppose I could call Dad, but he's got his own life now.

Yeah, I'll pick up some hours over the winter. They're bound to want extra help with the prep for Christmas. And then I'll just figure it out. It's gonna be okay, Char. It's all gonna be more than OK, it's gonna be great.

My stop is coming up. Cxx

With college over, I dated a few pillocks back in the day who, in hindsight, thought they could tame me. They were the sneaky ones. It all started well, in all the ways you expect a reasonable relationship to start, and then I somehow became too much. Too loud, too sexy, too magnetic, and they wanted me to rein myself in as if I couldn't be two things at once.

The pattern for me went like this: "Wow! Having a wild woman as your girlfriend is alluring. She's different; she pulls people in, especially one who is on the stage and who everyone looks at." But then, somewhere off-stage, when she has the confidence to tell your mate to stop getting handsy at the bar with a girl he doesn't know and who can hardly stand, she hits a level of attention that is too much. Or there were the ones that wanted to overprotect me, like I was a fragile bird. That wasn't going to work either, because I wasn't a broken bird when they met me; if anything I was still pretending to be an alley cat. Safer that way; birds end up a pile of feathers forgotten in the long grass.

The problem, which I see now is women are never designed to be one single thing or one version of themselves. Sometimes I'm loud and bubbly, other times I want to sit with my headphones curled up in a ball and cry to my favourite album, just because the world seems like a really horrible place that day. I hadn't found a boy or man that could hold all versions of me and my voice yet.

At almost 19, I went to London once for a long weekend to spend time with a guy I was seeing. We went shopping, and I bought a denim skirt for that night. We got back to the house to get ready and, after a shower, I got dressed, only to receive the comment, "Everyone's going to stare at you in that." No further context; just a simple statement. Didn't this guy meet me on a stage? Didn't he see the type of clothes I was wearing before this weekend? DId it really matter what I wore? Had I time travelled back to French class and not noticed?

Inside, my excitement shattered. I was meeting his friends for the first time in less than an hour, and I was miles away from home. My single remaining chord of confidence responded and said, "Let them." I smiled and applied my lipgloss before heading for the door. But something inside me was already mentally back on the train home. And that's how my relationship patterns were for a long while.

It started small as if they were testing the water: "You should wear these types of sunglasses," or "Why don't you colour your hair back to blonde? I liked it that way." You know how young men think they are helping you when it's just fulfilling a fantasy they have of you in their heads? There was a lot of that. I unknowingly and ever-so-slowly began to change at first. The problem was that once you start not to be true to yourself, you slowly begin to forget who you were in the first place. It starts small and slowly you begin to no longer recognise yourself in the mirror or hear your own voice in a conversation.

In the years following, I had a series of relationships where I tried to tame myself with smaller gigs, less performance, and less loudness, and neither was ideal nor very well-balanced. There was one guy who couldn't kiss with his eyes closed, or he would fall over; he cheated on me in a hotel one night after work while I was away on holiday. I don't tell you this out of pity. I tell you this because I was loud, I was raised by a woman who told me "Men will hurt you", and I still ended up here. It can happen easily and it can happen to anyone if you don't have discernment.

The next gaslit me into changing myself as often as he changed records at work. Over and over, I was giving up the one thing I said I would never sacrifice; bending myself to fit into someone else's box rather than us building a life together. When we are young, we often fall into the idea of love rather than the person in front of us. I didn't just fall, I drowned in it and in that I forgot my original intention: to find someone who loved me entirely.

As I've gotten older, my love life has taught me that some people's love can only carry you through a single phase of life, as if the love runs out when you become a new version of yourself, and that's OK. It is sad at times, but still, we quite literally live and learn. I often wonder if I fell in love with people who needed love, rather than people that could love me back. But then I remind myself we often do a lot of things when we are young that we may never fully understand. We have to let them go and keep moving forward.

Deep down under this shield, I was hoping there was a better version of the word love I had yet to experience. Because, despite the violence, manipulation, and gaslighting, somewhere inside I still believed in real love, a love that is true in its simplest form giving you wings to fly and a home that always feels safe.

Heart Thread — Love teaches us just as much, if not more, than fear does. The voice of Love comes in many forms; even the toxic types teach us something. I've dated some idiots in my time. I never regret knowing it was their loss for letting me go or leaving. We all deserve love, and we must believe it will find us. The thing we often forget to work out is what love looks like and feels like to us. It's often more different than we realise. Can love be painful? Yes, but not time and time again.

THE LANGUAGE I HAD TO LEARN

Wiping my finger under my eyelashes in the back room, hoping no one noticed the redness of my eyes and shadows from zero sleep. I was on a break from the late night shift for the new season store layout. One of the girls we called Bambi asked what I was writing about as she sat down with a box of cheesy goodness. I slipped my journal into my bag and shrugged my shoulders; she paused undeterred and waiting.

I stumbled for words. "Umm, sometimes I write about my day, other times I write myself a letter, like.. the words I wish someone would say to me, I guess. Most of the time I don't think, I just let the pen lead me." She flipped open the pizza box as the rest of my team walked in, and everything was forgotten, which I was grateful for as I had just written my heart out on the page.

He's gone. He took the last of his stuff and hasn't texted me begging again.

I feel heavy and light at the same time. I thought he loved me; he said he did over and over last night, and I cried because I knew he did. But it's not enough; it was never enough, even when I tried my hardest to make it work. Where did I go wrong?

My pen seemed to have a life of its own, and the words scribbled across the page.

He didn't love you as well as he could or should have. Don't forget that you deserve to be treasured in the ways of the stories you love. You deserve for your words to be listened to on and off stage. You deserve to have relationships where you feel honoured and never used or taken advantage of.

Love is about trust, which can be challenging at first or even in the middle, but it is all that matters in the end. Love cannot be forced, moulded, or made into something that fits. It flows like the ocean and changes back and forth as the tide does, this is love between two people over time. Push it to be something that it's not, and one of you will drown.

Learn the lessons of love child — For it is always available to you.

This was one of those relationships that had died a slow and quiet death. He was messaging a girl he worked with, and I think I had mentally closed off my heart months before when he pinned me up against the kitchen wall by my throat because I dared to speak a truth everyone knew but avoided. The morning I found their conversations on the laptop – reading the words he had written to her whilst I slept right next to him – gave me the momentum to demand that he leave before I got home from work that day.

I threw myself into my own work in hopes of distracting myself from the newfound quietness of the flat and wasn't interested in dating in the slightest. I was purely focused on my own needs. Four weeks later, I met up with a guy I went to school with. Ashley.

I had no intention of getting into anything serious with anyone at the time. I just knew I trusted him, he made me laugh and I had known him forever.

It would be a harmless coffee and a catch-up. Eight hours and one very late taxi ride home later, I wasn't as convinced we would only be friends as I was when I arrived.

After two dates, I remember reading his text saying he wanted to call me his girlfriend. I scoffed and replied to his message: "That's really nice of you to say, but I think you should go on your lads' holiday and see how you feel when you get back. Maybe we can catch up then." I clicked send and went off to the shop floor to give my team the morning brief from head office. When I returned, my phone flashed: "ONE NEW MESSAGE."

It read: "I don't need to go to Magaluf and back to know I'm never losing you again." And right there, I knew. I knew he was my person. He pushed through my walls with one line, refused to settle, and most importantly, in that tiny moment, he fought for me, which no one had done until then. I constantly brushed people off, playing the brave card with my quick wit and 'I don't need anybody' attitude. Twenty years later, he continues to fight for me.

Edgar Allen Poe once said: "Tell me every terrible thing you ever did, and let me love you anyway." And that is exactly what Ashley did. He has seen me at my worst, at my weakest, and at my most rageful at the world, and I have never, not for one second, doubted that seeing those parts of me would stop him from loving me.

He loves me for my too-muchness and by seeing that, I somehow began to love it a little as well. I know they say you have to learn to love yourself before you love another, on some level I did and I agree. But those final parts of me that I felt ashamed about, he taught me to love them in the deepest and yet most simple of ways.

I've known Ashley since I was eleven. We went to the same school, and in fact, we were considered boyfriend and girlfriend on a school trip to Paris when we were 12 years old. He had the pleasure of letting me sleep on his shoulder for the eight-hour coach ride home. I won't tell you how it ended — that's his favourite story to tell at parties. And I don't remember it. So, if he ever tells you, please bear in mind that I have no recollection of those events. But somehow, through some twist of fate or magic, we found each other again. And since that first cup of tea, we haven't left each other's side.

3rd July 2009 — Letter to self

Tomorrow you get married! Remember all those years that you swore you would never get married and yet the day you never thought would arrive is here!

I hope tonight you take a deep breath and let yourself feel everything — the excitement, the nerves, the joy. Allow yourself to be loved Char, know that you are worthy of it all. Everything you ever wanted or wished something would see in you. He sees it.

A new chapter, a new beginning with someone who adores you.

Don't worry, marriage isn't about everything being perfect — it's about choosing each other, every day. Love is the single reason to keep showing up and trying. Give it daily, give it with your words and your actions.

Tomorrow, you walk down that aisle towards years of laughter through the good and the bad. Remember that you are deeply loved — not just by Ashley, but by all of us who have been lucky enough to know you. I'll be cheering you on with so much love and pride. You did the one thing you struggled to do, you let someone see the real you, and guess what? They love you, because who wouldn't?!

Now get your rest, because we all know you don't want to wake up with puffy eyes for your big day.

Here's to forever beginning tomorrow. I love you.

I woke the morning of our wedding to hear the rain coming down in buckets. As I opened the curtains and looked out across the garden in the countryside, I listened to the kettle boiling, and could tell by the creaking of the floorboards that Ashley had noticed I was up early. I sat, curled up in my pink fluffy dressing gown at the farm-style dining table, watching him prep food like the pro in the kitchen; a sprinkle of this, a shake of that.

I smiled, watching him handle the knife carelessly, knowing that if the roles were reversed he'd be freaking out, telling me to stop talking and focus before I lose a finger.

Everyone else in the house was still deep in slumber – no surprise, given that it was before five. I padded out into the hallway and let my mind wander to how we'd set up the chairs later for the ceremony. I glanced over the sideboard where the stack of wildflower seed paper favours lay. My feet and thoughts led me into the living room, imagining all the families who had gathered around the open fire and those who would, for years, feel safe here in this little haven.

A blackbird's familiar song broke through my thoughts and I realised the rain had stopped. I opened the window and inhaled a deep breath of morning air, but it didn't quite hit the spot. With the puppy at my feet, I opened the big double doors into the garden and let the morning dew kiss my bare feet. The blackbird, now perched on the back of the patio chair, gave a little nod, which I, of course, returned with a quiet, "Good Morning Bobby."

A lump rose in my throat as I remembered how my grandad would always call our feathered friends Bobby Blackbird. I smiled through the tears, knowing he wouldn't be with us in person today as Bobby flew over the hedge and across the lane.

Every fibre knew this was one of my life's best and biggest decisions. Years from now, I'd tell my children that I knew their father was the one for me the first time I sat on his sofa at Willow Walk. They'd look at me with wide eyes and ask how I knew, and I'd tell them: "Easy. He didn't give me a single butterfly. He made me feel safe and calm in a way I hadn't felt in a very long time, something I didn't think I would find until I met him."

I shook my head as if to pull myself back from another emotional well, but then I heard my best friend Debbie's familiar voice at the top of the stairs: "Char, what are you doing up so early?!"

I laughed, turned around, and we squealed, "Because I'm/you're getting married!"

The day went like most weddings, with family drama, disagreements, and much dancing and drinking. But just before midnight, as we stood on top of the garden — me, Ashley, and our six-month-old puppy — we toasted the first day of our marriage.

As I write this now, I remember reading somewhere that rain on your wedding day is good luck. Something about how tying the knot on a rainy day symbolises that your marriage will last because a knot is hard to untie once it gets wet. With or without the rain, I know this knot is bound together across lifetimes.

The first few years were the hardest. I came to recognise that marriage isn't the gateway to happiness that so many describe. It's a gateway to growth and expansion, both together and individually. And with it comes a whole new bundle of emotions, dreams, and ideas.

Early on, I realised there weren't many great examples of marriage around us. So we decided to throw our ideas on the table and mix them up. We went through that bumpy road of judging other people's marriages (we all do it, even if we pretend we don't), and as time passed, we've also learned to pull ideas from marriages that we admire, make them work for us until we created new ways of our own.

THE CHORUS OF A FAMILY

Over the years, through clients, partners, friends, and various communities, I've seen so many different kinds of families. Each one with its own patterns, traditions, rhythms, and energy.

Family culture and tradition are often the invisible hand that sets the tone, tempo, expectations. Not a single person, but a force. No two are ever the same. As a teen I had thrown myself into the vibe of my boyfriend's family only to realise that they weren't as welcoming or as honest as they first seemed; when I got comfortable enough to honour my own rhythm I was shunned or shamed for not making it easy for my boyfriend.

More often than most I spoke as I felt and saw, they however seemed to speak quite differently behind my back as they did to my face and this left me another gaping hole of mistrust around love, however luckily for me, I grew a thicker skin over the years.

Every family has their own little ways: how they start conversations or avoid them, who they call first when trouble comes, how they handle grief, welcome new family members, or even something as simple as celebrating a birthday. I've spent time in homes where the matriarch or patriarch, the one whose influence carries the most weight, sets the tone. What they say goes and it doesn't matter if it's right or wrong. Everyone else stays quiet so as not to disturb the "peace." I've seen parents hold the reins so tightly their kids barely whisper. I've watched families hide things from their grandparents just to keep the false sense of calm.

I've heard men talk to their wives as if they were nothing but dirt under a shoe. And I've also been lucky enough to sit in homes where the whole family's voice is one warm, beautiful circle of love; it makes me tear up just thinking of it. And then there are the houses that look perfect from the outside, but behind closed doors, there's no harmony at all.

The first time I really stopped to think about what I wanted my own family to look like was one Christmas I spent with Ashley, long before we were married. We divided the day between two households, moving from one to the other, and I remember noticing the contrast – how different homes carried such different feelings. That day opened my eyes, and ever since I've paid attention to the ways our families move and live together.

Let's be clear here, no family is perfect, including my own, though most of us possibly aren't even aware of it until someone crosses the threshold from the outside and joins or interlinks another family. So who's the voice of a family? Is it the man of the household? The grandparents? The oldest sibling? Who leads? No one or everyone? Does a family function without a clear leader?

When each person thinks they're conducting or is fighting to control the rhythm of lineage? And how does that work when you branch off and have your own family? These are all questions I wish I had a clear and final answer to, but all I can tell you is what I have so far.

Let's use choirs as a metaphor here for families, we could have used this for the entire book, and yet it feels more potent if we plant it here at the doormats of the homes we grew up in.

When we leave our birth choir we often leave with a voice full of borrowed notes, and then we try to write our own melody which often feels at the beginning unfinished in ways, but it's yours and that's what counts.

Most of the time in families there is no conductor, just the long echo of tradition keeping time. We might witness many people attempt to stand in the pit and conduct, and yet even as they move their hands in some sort of tempo, is it really theirs? Or is it the tempo of their parents, or the song of their great great grandparents whose voices are low and unwavering, shaped by hard winters, war, and rules they never thought to question. Can you hear it?

Their harmonies are so tight, they are almost rigid. You don't improvise in their key. You blend, or you fall silent. As your parents conduct, waving invisible batons. They raised their voices not to be heard, but to hold the line. Some days they sang in unison; other days, they clashed like brass and drum. They wanted order in the chaos, but they'd forgotten the melody they were meant to follow.

And then there are the children who sing too loud or too soft, a little off-key and out of time. Some of us screamed our solos, just desperate to be heard. Others mouthed the words with no sound at all. I remember one cousin who always tried to harmonise, really tried, but could never quite find the note. Even when her father snatched her voice, still, she kept singing. That mattered.

Then you become a teenager, new families join through marriage or chance and everyone acts as if they'd missed rehearsal. Sometimes we resent how their notes bent our family's tune. But if you listen closely, sometimes the song gets better. Fuller. Strange chords at first, but more honest somehow. New singers in a choir often give us more depth but also a better chance of seeing where we need to work.

Eventually some of us leave. pack our sheet music and start our own choirs, in living rooms and apartments, with lullabies and morning arguments. We carry the old melodies in our bones, even when we swore we wouldn't. Even when we write new songs. And, like so many of us, though I never asked for it, I became a choirmaster. Hesitant at first, then steadier, guiding voices I helped bring into the world, praying that I'd teach them not just to sing, but to listen.

Because every family is a choir. Not always in harmony, not always in tune. But still a song.

THE OFF NOTES OF EARLY MARRIAGE

I have known women say my husband is one of the best men they know. I often think my husband sees me as some sort of Selkie who may eventually return to the sea and leave him forever. And I'm getting this out in the open now because I need to be honest with you: He is the best man I've ever known and also, he is loud as hell. But I still see us as two kids leaning on each other, facing this long journey. I keep a picture of us as kids in my journal, so when I want to rip his eyeballs out I can look at it and remember we are just two kids trying to figure it out.

You see, he takes up space in a way I've never experienced before. I'm not talking about some ignorant man on the train who is man-spreading, I mean in the way he shows up in the world. He doesn't care what people think, he doesn't care how tidy the house is when someone comes over. He's always unapologetically himself. Even the way he walks across the landing as if playing the role of a giant in *Jack and the Beanstalk* used to drive me up the wall. The noise, the space he takes up and with not a single drop of shame.

How I hadn't noticed this before we were married I don't know. At first, I didn't see the whole picture through our early marriage hurdles. But then, I wondered: Why can't I do that too?

We've learned to coax words from each other, sometimes with long, well-crafted texts when my emotions run so high you can't even understand the words through the snot and tears. We've had long nights or car rides planning how we want our world to look. Creating the voice of a family takes practice, but through it all — tears and awkward conversations included — we figure it out.

So one day, I asked him, "How come you walk around the house so loudly, and you don't seem bothered about what people think?"

He didn't take his eyes off the road and asked, "OK, random. Firstly, why'd you ask?"

Scrunching my face, I said, "I'm just not sure I can do that. Something in me won't allow it, almost."

He softly laughed and said, "I think the better question is what idiot told you you can't. And secondly, when have *you* ever felt the need to ask for permission for anything?" I looked out the passenger window as far left as possible, as I always do when I need to cry.

Something so simple to him felt so impossibly hard for me. Was it the difference in how we were raised? It could be more significant than that. I didn't know at the time. But all I could do was keep chipping away at who I thought I needed to be until I returned to the person I was born to be.

It's funny how we often move in different worlds. He's ex-military, raised in a family with a significant military background, and works in corporate. I'm a free-spirited wild woman who often talks about things I can see that others don't. When I say I need to climb the moors or spend a day at a castle with a friend, he never hesitates to support me. We may live in different worlds often but, like magnets, we always pull back together at the end of each day.

We all have hang-ups, habits and triggers; internally, this is where the real battle begins. We often blame our partner, but I also have some patterns to break. I'm super independent, a little stubborn, and love a plan. I married a man who is laid back and takes things as they come. If you need him to do something, you just ask. However, for so long I was so independent and mistrusting of people that I didn't even know how to ask for help.

I was so independent for so long that it almost became a part of my personality shield. I trusted him with my life, yet it took me longer than I cared to share to reprogram my brain to see I wasn't doing life alone. Having the wrong people in my life for long had taught me that I could do it all on my own, whereas Ashley knew I *could*, but he had to keep reminding me that I didn't need to try to keep doing it myself.

On the outside, these can be small things, like not smacking the new chutney jar lid with a wooden spoon until you hear the seal pop and instead just taking it to the living room and asking him to open it. It can also be more significant, like not sitting in silence after someone has hurt me; sharing it with him, and not feeling weak or less of a partner by being emotional or hurt by something a friend had said or done. I had to learn that my emotions were not an inconvenience and the flow of them didn't make me any less of a life partner.

I was a 'parentified daughter', so I had to start small; not sugar-coating my day, asking for him to take the reins when I felt exhausted, and being able to say I didn't have the answers to everything, no matter how organised my plan was. And of course healing my deepest childhood wound by trusting that he wouldn't leave, no matter how emotional or weird things got.

I began to work on these things layer by layer, and those layers are a constant process. Starting early was possibly a good thing, as they were only going to get stranger as the years passed.

Through years of marriage, we've learned that clear communication is vital but it's not enough; respect and boundaries matter just as much. Even as a team, we are still two separate souls, walking side by side up this metaphorical mountain. Some things are not up for discussion in public and we constantly check in with each other, not out of fear but to keep the channels open. Because if there's one thing I know for sure, it's this: as soon as communication stops, everything else starts to fall apart.

That doesn't just apply to romantic relationships, it's true for all. Lack of communication leaves room for confusion, misinterpretation, and resentment to creep in. It's why we've learned to embrace clarity, and over-explain when necessary until we hit the core of what's really happening.

Sometimes we need to preface deep or awkward conversations to ensure how we are feeling is clear and make sure our words land the way we intend. Because, in the end, relationships need our voices. Without them, nothing works.

Each time, we have to pull ourselves back and share another layer of what we are thinking or, most importantly, feeling. However, let's be clear; sometimes, it goes beyond words. I'll give him what he calls 'the wide eye', and he will say "I feel like I said I would do something, and I have forgotten," or, "What's the look for?"

And me? My favourite thing to do is leave the kitchen cupboards open late at night, so when he gets up before sunrise and walks into the kitchen, his first thought is that we have been burgled. The first time was an accident; I had unloaded the dishwasher before bed and just kind of forgot. Now, though, I just do it for fun. There is nothing like an early morning fright to keep the love alive!

We still drive each other up the wall; we don't argue but debate regularly and though what works for us has taken time to cultivate, we know it may change again at some point.

I've often been asked what the secret to success in marriage is. I always smile because deep down, we know that success is one of those vague words, defined by not only each couple but each person. But honestly? I think the secret is this: You both need to keep improving. In a great marriage, you have love, safety, and support. But what matters is accepting constant growth, because you will keep changing and evolving. Nothing ever stays the same as much as we wish it would.

And above all, friendship. He's my best friend, and every time I forget that – which I sometimes do, like when struggling to concentrate on writing this while he's singing off-key at the top of his voice across from the kitchen table; or the times he uses the big light when I'm reading a book, all snuggly and relaxed before bed and I swear to him when we buy our forever home, I am having a guy come in and permanently remove all ceiling lights because we are a small light household!

Then there are times he will curse when he dies on *Call of Duty* and blame my bad juju, or I will catch him wincing when I get super loud and excitable because he has sensitive ears. We are human, but above all we always want what is best for each other. If there comes a time when you no longer want good things for your partner, then usually the damage is already done.

Laughter is key, meaning learning to laugh at yourself more than others; let's not get mean here. I've lost count of the times I've had to laugh at myself and apologise, but sometimes, that's all that is needed, ownership of your actions. Do we fall out? Of course, all the time. But love is not always gentle. Sometimes, it's sharp around the edges, but it keeps trying. Love is always trying.

Heart Thread — The most profound relationships require a combination of things that root from a centre of respect, communication and compromise. The moment you start to see yourself as on separate teams, it goes wrong. The voice of the best relationships are collaborative. All the C's it would seem. They are combined over time, not through fear but through trust.

THE MACHINE I HAD TO LEAVE

At the beginning of my corporate career I had all these visions of making a significant change in the working world, being valued for my skills and humour, and being noticed for the energy I could bring to projects. I believed my time on the stage and in adult environments for the past nine years gave me not only a good working relationship with older people, but also an edge.

Maybe I'd watched too many American movies and series by that point. Because what I found in most jobs was a battle with hierarchy and a lack of support from management. Work environments have many voices and every single one of them wants to be heard. It's often like a really unorganised or poorly led choir.

My first part-time job was as a waitress at a local golf course. It paid just over six pounds an hour, which wasn't great, especially when I could earn more than triple that singing. I can't remember why I took the job; maybe it was the adult environment or the unlimited supply of cocktail cherries. But when the boss made a couple of inappropriate jokes about my body and smacked my ass with a clipboard, I put him in his place. After that shift I vaguely remember him telling my friend who had got me the job that there were no more shifts left for me.

Do you remember the greeters at Asda? I'm unsure if they still have them, but that was my second role, and I was one of the best in the South West! Or that's what I told myself at that age. My job was simple: greet everyone as they entered the store, announce special offers or staff updates, flirt with Graham in the music and video section when the managers weren't looking, and lock up at the end of the night.

The part I loved most about this job (there wasn't much) was the sense of community with people who came through the front door. I watched babies learn to walk, joked with customers and made friends. It was as if, for the first time, I could see the community I had grown up in. I saw my friends' grandparents come in like clockwork and watched the world go by from the entryway of that store. Then I moved into the offices as the Events Coordinator.

I adored the idea of this role, when I was actually allowed to do it, rather than being dragged to checkouts to cover someone else's lunch and delay my own. I was in local schools doing community presentations or supporting local charity events.

Within a year working upstairs I was sat in a team meeting on Thursday afternoon. Eight or nine of the team were in their thirties or forties, while I was about twenty. Our new manager was out sick, and we had been given a stand-in manager to lead the meeting. I was asked to keep some notes in case we needed them.

I obliged, took my notebook out of my bag, and began to write brief notes on the topics as they came up. We didn't usually have notes taken in these types of meetings, so I wasn't overly worried. However, the concerns began coming thick and fast across the meeting room. Department heads demanding the admin go to support different departments and then wondering why work wasn't completed on time, etc., the usual, I thought. Then the topic switched to the manager, who was currently out sick. Suddenly, everyone was throwing their opinions in at her lack of support, the fact that she was rarely available for them or out of the office, etc. In my hazy mind, I wrote in my notepad: "*Let's all slag off Toni!!!!! They do not speak for me.*"

I still laugh at my boldness, but as I sat there, I was consumed by a rage that no fireproof blanket would extinguish. I liked my new boss. She was always available for me; she supported rather than ignored me but she was different, and that's not always liked. Especially in a building where we are handing out flowers for people who have been there for almost 30 years. They had employed externally for once, and she was already coming up against internal walls. As the youngest on the team, I knew what that was like.

I knew she was working on system reviews and trying to bring in a fresh perspective, and the fact the women around the room didn't see this wasn't important to me – what *was* important was that I had sat in these meetings and never seen anyone bring these things up with her or her manager. Yet somehow, now it had become a bit of a mud-slinging match.

In my head, I wasn't going to add my personal note to the final edit of notes, assuming someone might want an actual hard copy. Now, here was my significant error. I placed my notepad on the desk while I took a large gulp of water from my bottle. At that point, the colleague next to me saw my notes. I knew immediately I was in trouble.

Let me tell you, I took those steps from the meeting as if I were a gazelle being chased by a cheetah. Flying to my office and towards my desk in hopes of some correction fluid, now realising someone might actually want a copy of the worst meeting I have ever attended.

Within two minutes, the manager who had taken the meeting called me into the empty office at the end of the corridor. She asked me where my notes were. I said on my desk; I would get them typed up before the end of the day and put a copy in her tray. She smiled and asked me to get my notebook.

What followed felt like walking the green mile. I returned with my now edited notes and handed them to her. She let out a long sigh, pointed to the line I had covered, and asked, "What did this part say exactly?" I looked her in the eye and said: "That bullet point said 'Let's slag off Toni.'" "Is that what you think we did today?" she asked.

With shaking hands, I nodded and said: "Unless it's a formal complaint about another staff member, I don't think we should be having group discussions about a manager with one of her colleagues. And if I'm honest I don't agree with what was said."

She placed the notebook on the table. "This company-owned stationery is not what it is meant to be used for!" I smiled and informed her that it was mine as I bought it with my own money, as the stationary budget for my department was almost zero.

At this point, I think she was done with me. With a firm warning not to let this happen again, she sent me back to my desk, I think it was at this moment that I became certain I was not going to last long in an HR office.

I was never asked for the meeting minutes, but I would warn Toni the next time she came in. She returned for a short time and then left for a better job, not before returning the favour and warning me that the woman who had my job before me was repeatedly asking if she could return to my position. We often blame men for many of the issues in the work place, but from what I have experienced women functioning in their competitive masculine are just as bad, if not worse. I also played that game for a few years. It doesn't work.

Work life, for me, was always going to be a storm in a teacup. I'd overproduce, then either take over from a boss or get promoted, and eventually fall from grace. Sometimes, this was my fault, other times it was just a combination of circumstances. Over the years, I've worked everywhere from admin desks, retail and management, and I've probably seen it all.

Men who talked over me, women intimidated rather than inspired by my youth; there was even one colleague who sent daily emails about me to the lady who had left and whose role I had taken over, only to forget to delete them from the reception desk before I sat down. Reading those over my morning cuppa each day was a real way to fuel my day. Let's remind you here, I needed no extra fire.

Very quickly, I learned that not all wolves follow you into the woods; some just sit at the desk next to you, pulling the strings and whispering behind your back. It didn't matter how many Becky's, Kristina's or Beverley's I met along the way, because for every woman who would burn another to save herself there was one who had used her voice for change; women who rebuilt systems or simply brought a different energy to the office that lightened the heavy load that was corporate.

Jane Redman, Heather Cowan, Gaynor Norman and Debbie Williams. They were, for me, women who showed up to make a difference; not to compete but to encourage. They'd often kick my butt or as Jane would say "give them enough rope they'll hang themselves" and for years, that's exactly what I did. I took on projects, extra work and responsibility and I ended up hanging myself time and time again.

Corporate gave me some of the best stories of my life, like the time a commando rolled under store shutters and I had to run round to the other side of the carpark to fix my error and pray no one saw me. I'm sure security had a laugh at that footage in the morning. However if there was a story that showed my commitment to work but also the hilariousness that is my life it would be the day I got locked in the house on my first day at a new job.

I had just moved into a house with Ashley and his sister. Sharing the space while he was at camp Monday through Friday made sense.

Ashley was heading back to work from a nearby regiment, and I was preparing for my new job in the office at an insurance car repair company in Bath. I got ready as usual – nervous but with plenty of time. However, I hadn't anticipated the winter weather swelling the wooden front door from all the rain and though I pulled with all my might, it wouldn't budge.

I even leaned out the front window and asked an elderly gentleman walking his dog to help push it from the outside while I pulled, but still, the door was having none of it. I couldn't leave through the back door either, as it didn't lock from the outside, and that would've meant sudden death at the hands of Ashley's sister. (We hadn't lived together long when this happened, but if this was today I'd probably risk it, leave the back door unlocked, lock the gate and run for the bus. But then I suppose that's often the case with some of life's best stories.)

I called the one person I knew would always pick up: Ashley. To say he wasn't thrilled about the situation would be an understatement. By this point, I had already missed my bus. Could I call my new job and explain that I was locked in the house on my first day? Would they believe me? I wouldn't believe it if someone else called me with that story. Could I lose a job without even starting? Was this some kind of extreme test? I was emotional on the end of the phone, pushing down tears.

Ashley told me to hang tight and have breakfast; he'd be there soon. Whenever I tell this story, I imagine his massive army truck doing a U-turn just before hitting the motorway. And sure enough, the unmistakable sound of a four-tonne military truck pulling into our quiet cul-de-sac followed by Ashley in full uniform, who managed to open the door with one brute push of his shoulder. The relief I felt was overwhelming.

I checked the bus timetable; I'd be nearly an hour late if I got the next bus, and waiting for a taxi might be even longer; that wasn't going to work. So, in the middle of my panic, Ashley devised the solution: he'd drive me in the truck. There I was, perched between the driver and passenger seats, handbag on my lap, heels on, wedged between two engineers heading to central Bath.

We arrived as half the company's paint shop were outside with their morning coffees, and the other half stood at the breakfast van. Ashley's colleague opened the door for me and I attempted to exit gracefully in my heels, only to see that he wasn't on the ground... oh no, instead he had chosen to hang from the truck by one arm like some sort of action man.

The embarrassment of showing up to work with a military escort on my first day was real. But to my surprise, not a single person in the body shop ever turned down a request that came from my desk, because you don't mess with the girl in the office that had a military escort to her first day on the job.

Over the years I've been involved in takeovers and buyouts. I showed up to a new office on the Monday of the merging week and was placed in a dusty cupboard with two colleagues for over a month because "there wasn't any other space." Nothing says "welcome to the merger" like working in a windowless box with no windows and broken chairs.

I've been in meetings where I repeatedly struggled to keep my face neutral and was told time and time again that I questioned too many things, especially when they seemed to dance on the edge of being unethical; and the higher I got, the harder it became. I rubbed management up the wrong way with my quick tongue and moral high ground, though I tried to keep hold of it for as long as possible. I don't think I realised how much I had lost of myself between the promotions and pay rises. Until I noticed that the cracks began to appear in my team, and that was not a good sign.

Despite the fact I didn't think or work the way people often wanted me to, my dedication to being employed was never in question. However, work for me was always a disappointing arena where people seemed to forget that we all wanted the same thing. Until I myself forgot this, the voice I thought was my own became awash with corporate beliefs and focused on figures and profits.

Corporate systems seem to have a way of pulling us in with promises of a mission, only to mould us into something unrecognisable. I didn't even realise the inner conflict they caused me for years. Trying to be a good person, change the system, and still get the pay cheque for all the hard work is impossible for someone like me who feels everything deeply.

The world of work does that though, doesn't it? Slowly blurs your vision until you aren't only the mouthpieces of the company, but you are also wearing the company-branded glasses and can't remember how you even got there.

After years, I realised I'd lost many parts of myself to corporate. It reshaped me in ways I didn't notice until it was too late. Every place I worked took something from me until I wasn't even a person I liked anymore. From 9-5 I was speaking in someone else's tongue – the company lingo down to a tee. And out of hours my words became bitter, frustrated, and lost in my anger, until I left.

Over time, I've seen corporate as an old paradigm; a silent killer of souls. It doesn't suit me, in fact I'm not sure it suits many people, it's just that we have been led to believe we have no other choice but to work ourselves to the bone until retirement.

We all know that the corporate voice is sly and yet all we seem to say is "that's just the way it is." A structure that preaches community and family values, but the pressure to hit targets and meet sales quotas overrides equality and intention and we the people keep not only buying but showing up, despite knowing better?

It's so easy to blame the corporate world on men when they so dominate it, but actually, it's so often the women who get sucked into the rusty cogs of this outdated system the world seems to revolve around; and when we leave we seem to forget to sit in the fact we think nothing of selling our voices and our energy to the next highest bidder.

I will also hold my hands up to my behaviour as I began feeding the system I never wanted to be a part of. Which means for me, in my experience we must talk about older women as well.

In my early twenties I was the one who pulled teams together. I'd jump on a train to support another practice manager, brimming with new ideas on how to make life easier and more efficient, only to feel unwelcome and met with resistance. As someone who's now been on the receiving end of that energy, let me tell you – it sucks on either side. Solutions are only made when both parties are honest about it. God, I wished people just communicated clearly instead of putting on this 'professional' mask.

As older women in any environment we really need to learn to welcome a fresh pair of eyes and new ideas, rather than feel intimidated and bring up a wall of defence with lines like "That won't work here".

The work mask I chose cost me friends and a little part of my soul. I once remember seeing a message from our receptionist about me to another team member. One of these women I had gotten this job, and a career pathway within the company. We hung out at weekends and here she was calling me a bitch and when I saw these words I couldn't help but question if this was true.

Had I become a bitch or would my managerial requests have landed differently if I were a man? Bette Davis once said "When a man gives his opinion, he's a man. When a woman gives her opinion she's a bitch" So I continued and hoped I could keep at least a small part of the woman I was before I became a cog in the machine that was never built for women or designed to let us speak.

Not long after I swallowed the truth that you cannot change the world within its existing systems. I should have left, built a new structure to work from. Instead of creating change, I let a stack of industries change me, losing not only my voice but my way.

I messed up. Like truly messed up. In my mid-twenties, I slid into a job at a dental practice. I made some of the biggest mistakes there and still feel ashamed of many of them. I've taken things that weren't mine or meant for me, including jobs, all whilst slowly forgetting the original intention of why I wanted to go out into the working world.

Yet the biggest one on the list, the one at the top, was not speaking out from the beginning and allowing the work environment I was supposed to manage to become ever so toxic right before my eyes.

A lot of that was on me, and I lost count of the hours of sleep I lost when I left that place. Had I been too loud? Did I choose the wrong team? Or did I think I could remain friends with those I now had to manage? Did my monthly team newsletter seem too friendly, "as if I was talking to a friend and not leading the team"?

I often found myself down one of two routes at work: I either left the position immediately in a cloud of dramatic smoke, or took over a higher management role to end up quickly resenting that position and the place of work in its entirety.

Much like Gandalf, I continued to disturb the peace in most jobs I took. Suppose there is an unspoken word in the room, a faint whiff of the unspoken; if I believed it would shift things for the better within the company when it was said, then I was the girl to say it. I would leave jobs under a dark cloud, and the most common theme was that I didn't feel heard. My voice was used, but it wasn't fully heard by the people I worked with or for.

The voice of corporate — not all, but most — needs a total rewrite. Or possibly it needs its infected tonsils removed so it can sing an entirely new tune. You'll often read that women need to take the helm, and rightly so. There need to be some heads that roll and a rather large shift in equality. I know this because I may have saved my soul from the corporate slog almost twenty years ago, but I still witness it and it still ripples into my household because it affects us much more widely than simply who pays our paycheck.

I always find this one difficult, because my husband still works in those wheels of the industry, and I see him fighting to this day for the small things: honesty, trust, and equality. Not being asked to lie, fixing numbers, and pretending you are a family when really you are a money-focused machine of the worst kind.

The hard truth is we need each other. Corporate pulls us into a false magnetism of petty competition and fighting for the promotion. And why? Because we are mistaking money for abundance. Money is so small, but it's also unfortunately important; an energy that we far too deeply connect to our self-worth. Why? Because the world told us that's how we measure it: by the possessions we have, the job title we were offered and the number of zeros in our bank account.

We forget about joy, love, passion, freedom, creativity and mystery; those aren't things we buy. No. Those are the avenues the world uses to sell. Clever, huh? When you suddenly look at selling through emotions you can see a lot about why we buy what we buy.

I personally don't buy what corporations are selling, and I say that energetically. The voice of corporate is selling from pain, building from patriarchy, and so focused on one thing: taking your money and feeding you into a spiral of debt and wanting that you may never get out of. That system is one I'll never sell my voice to again. I made the decision that my voice is my own, and if it was used for a brand or a company, it would be one I believed in. I knew this in my twenties, and I stand by it today.

I only wish I had removed my voice from all the answer machines before I walked out.

Heart Memo — Companies assume they own your voice when you are on their payroll. High-exposure projects like movies or brand partnerships online show us examples of this on a much larger scale. But often we forget about those of us in mainstream jobs are no different. Companies often expect those under their banner to align with the same beliefs, whether they are spoken or not. In these spaces, people often feel they must sanitise or shape their voices to keep jobs, appease employers, or fit into company "culture." But is your voice really yours if someone else controls how and when and how you use it?

Journal Entry 2023 —

Ashley's boss has told him they don't want him in Friday's meetings for a while and I am pisssed about it, but not surprised. His boss said "it's not the tone they want at the moment" and yet his boss's boss specifically asked for him to attend because he is the eyes and ears on the ground. (in short one of the few that drags himself away from his desk to go out on site and see with his own eyes and talk to the teams).

You know what the tone is that they don't really want? Truth. The tone they are avoiding is truth. Dates that they undoubtedly not be able to make, targets that some nodding dog has agreed to and had no consideration of external factors such as weather or the fact these are people doing the work not machines.

I hoped that corporate as a majority was changing, but today has reminded me it is very much the minority that are creating the change we need to see.

It's been twelve years since I worked in corporate and it's not changing fast enough.

Anyway, I just wanted to get my frustration out of my body. He's going to the meeting — of course he's going to the meeting. That's the type of man I married. But I am sad for him, I am sad for a world that has forgotten there are other ways to create outside of big corps, and that honesty should be welcome in every meeting.

Cx

THE ILLUSION OF ABUNDANCE

Heavily pregnant and having just walked out of my job, I began to worry about money. It's not that I had never worried about money before, I knew all too well what it was like growing up in the early years with a house whose finances were overseen by my Dad, an accountant; and the teenage years where I was very aware that I was the lucky one to have my own money coming in. But when you have a child inside of you, well the need for financial stability feels all the more important.

I was never really what you might call a big spender, I can't exactly remember when I first understood money, but as a child I do remember my mother shooing us out of the way when my Dad did the family accounts on a Sunday. I felt the energy in the house tighten as he sat there with a stack of receipts, while my mum would suddenly be very busy in other rooms.

I remember my dad working ridiculously hard, which he still does. I remember breakfasts in Tesco before the food shop on a Saturday morning and, sometimes, Friday night chip shop tea with my pineapple fritter and chips. We weren't rich, but from what I could understand we were sensible.

I always think money has several layers of voice, and they don't always gel easily together inside of our minds, which means we each carry an inner money conflict of layers that we don't tend to often explore. Our beliefs around cash often come from the patterns we are born into. We inherit ideas of money without even realising it. Sometimes, it's a case of our parents wanting more for us than they had.

Other times, it's more about climbing the ladder and paying it forward to future generations. Perhaps it's the town we live in, the history of our families, but I distinctly remember being shown two if not four very different examples of money in my childhood.

I watched my mother attempt to raise five children on and off over the years, and my father worked himself to the bone to provide until he left. Their divorce left my mother, in her eyes, to pick up the pieces. She remarried an abusive man with a drink problem and drummed into me from a young age that my father only cared about money.

Meanwhile my father remarried and had twins. Going on to become a CEO of a company, with a gorgeous house, while he and his wife also put their children through private school. For a long time I was able to witness a household that, from a distance, seemed to have a lot of money, while the household I was living in did not seem to have much at all. I saw the difference on every level.

Now unemployed I had a lot of time to think about the type of parent and wife I wanted to be. And I'm not talking surface level decisions about who will cook the tea, I'm talking about big decisions. Because for so long I was earning very good money and now? Well now I was pregnant and not making any money at all, and this made me feel quite useless. This was the beginning of feeling as if I was not contributing enough.

If I had to choose I'd rather be tighter on the purse strings than exhausted, bitter, and wavering in my morals. But the way I see it now is we shouldn't have to sacrifice either. There are ways we can have all the things if we build them carefully and if we trust.

The problem is I'm not sure that feeling ever fully disappears, when the world whispers that if we aren't rich we couldn't possibly be happy. And yet abundance can look like very different things to different people.

A few years ago my father said: "Just make sure you are doing all you can to support Ashley." I cried for about a week non-stop, because a small comment that meant no harm made me realise that women are supposed to be able to do it all and keep a smile on their faces. We are expected to work, clean, cook and raise children and support the money maker of the house.

Money is this whisper behind all things we do and it's rude to talk about salary or income on one hand; yet on the other, we love to share when we get a bargain, and the luxury lifestyle is constantly being sold to us as the desired end result for all. Could we start talking about both? Maybe we could release a little shame around it whilst we are there.

Sitting on my grandmother's sofa eating dark chocolate digestives and talking about her days when she lived in a country village, I decided money was great. I love money, but in our household, we were going to focus on joy and love. All the rest of it would follow, I was sure of it. They could call it hippy bull crap, but I wanted my daughter to grow up with parents who she got to spend time with and to never wonder if work was more important than she was.

I understood that money was only an exchange of energy that we have made palpable in paper and coin. And quite frankly there were also more important things in life, such as family connection, a safe home and joy. I waddled home that night with my mind swimming in money and my bank account the exact opposite.

Was ABBA right? Is it a rich man's world? Or is this something we have just been led to believe?

Later that night, curled up listening to a summer storm, trying to distract myself from the constant heartburn, I asked what the words 'success and abundance' meant to Ashley.

He talked about the basics. He'd set up a consultancy, I'd raise the children and be self-employed, we'd get an allotment to grow our own food while spending our spare time by the water or off on adventures in our camper van. I smiled on the outside, but my inside voices reminded me this wasn't how people did things. They worked their entire lives; they pushed people from positions they wanted. They charged ahead no matter what. I hushed the voice in my head and wondered if I could somehow block out yet another voice of society? Was it so wrong to let joy be our compass for life?

Heart Thread – The voice of money is one we think we know, yet it often takes up too much of our focus. What if we shifted our attention just a little toward what sparks joy, toward what lights us up inside? That is the pathway to abundance, not as the world narrowly defines it, but in the shape of our own lives.

Success, too, asks for this reframing. It isn't a final destination, nor a static prize to hold forever. It is movement like breath, like wind; shaping and reshaping us through obstacles, delays, and curveballs. True success makes space, invites flow, and expands possibility. Don't be fooled into thinking it only exists within rigid systems or old definitions that no longer serve. Abundance and success live in motion, in joy, and in the freedom to redefine them for ourselves.

Letter to self —

CHARLIE!! You are pregnant!! Congratulations!! I am so excited for you!

I wish you could see how your fire lights corners in rooms you are not even noticing. I wish you could feel as safe as you make others feel and I wish you could remember all of the people's lives you have changed, just by showing up as yourself.

I wish you could see that all those moments, even now, so young, you have made a difference and you deserve happiness.

Accomplishments are funny things — they may not be as shiny or as loud as the world tells you they are. But they prove (not that anything really ever needs to be proven),they show you that you have all the heart that it requires to be a great parent.

That feeling in your chest. The moments, the sparks and the fear. The feeling of overwhelming joy and fear. And the shame of not having it all planned or figured out — bringing a new soul into the world that often seems to be losing its way. It may never leave, but in the right months' time you will know it was worth it.

You will never have everything in its perfect place to bring a child into the world. The same way there is no perfect household or perfect marriage. These things are built and you, you are a master builder.

Build the life you dream of, not only for your child and your partner but for yourself. Xx

THE HANDS THAT HOLD MY HEART

For the entire duration of my pregnancy, I thought I was going to die in labour. This was one of the first times I didn't tell anyone how absolutely petrified I was. Not a friend, not my husband. If I'm honest I didn't see the point in sharing, knowing all anyone was going to say was: "Women have been doing this since the beginning of time, you'll be fine."

This was my belief before I entered the reality of the third trimester. I believed it was highly probable I wouldn't survive; my dreams showed me giving birth to my daughter and diminishing into cosmic dust at the same time. The only brief relief from that fear I can remember was the walk to work with my headphones on singing Soul Sister by train at the top of my lungs each morning.

Perhaps it was symbolic more than anything; a part of us does die when we give birth, and also an extension of us is born, a new voice that we have no control over, one that can 'out' us in a supermarket or one that could potentially turn around one day and use their words against us. Maybe it was that I didn't feel strong enough yet to defend the fragile life growing inside of me or capable of building the type of life they deserved?

Yet during those most powerful last few weeks, I could not, or would not, think past labour. I filled the wardrobe with freshly washed babygrows, I stocked up the baskets on the changing unit with wet wipes and cotton wool, and sometimes late at night, I would sit in the nursery looking at the little rows of tiny socks and mittens people had given us while wondering who would put them on her if I didn't make it.

I would silently cry and then push the tears down as the sun rose into the autumnal sky. I constantly tried to remind myself throughout the day that I was safe, I was healthy, I had no medical history that was a concern and that not all modern medicine was bad.. In a nutshell my first pregnancy was as if life and death were rubbing up against each other inside of me. Old me was dying and a new life was about to be birthed into the world.

Maybe I had a past life where this had happened. At the time, I couldn't be sure, so I wrote a letter to Ashley and my unborn child; I had always loved writing letters to myself or friends over the years. The first letter was many pages long, explaining what she needed to be taught and how I wanted her to be wild and sassy. I laugh now as I write this because she is precisely that, some days I wonder where she got it from, and then I remember: if I'm a spark, then that kid is a wildfire.In the letter, I asked Ashley to let her fly free always and give her a nest where she could land safely just as he had done for me.

The second letter was more of a welcome to the world letter, a letter that told her no matter how dark the world might seem, there was always light to be found, and that light was always worth looking for.

I told her our story so far, how we saw each other at school and then found each other again. I told her I would love her father beyond lifetimes and find them both again the next time round. Then, I left them in the front pocket of my hospital bag. A lily bobtail 'just in case pocket' if you will. To the outside world, I carried on as if all was well.

The midwife at my final appointment, although she didn't say it, clearly thought I had lost my mind. I believe she told me I was "a silly sausage", to be exact; she also happened to be the midwife who birthed me when I was born. We agreed not to focus on the possibility of death overly, and that if it was my time, then clearly, this was what I came here to do. Sue retired just before I gave birth and was replaced by another Sioux. I loved the first midwife, for we had a thread I could pull from childhood. But the second, she got me on a level that I needed. Thank the gods for midwives who listen to women and laugh with them when they are most vulnerable, especially for someone like me who back then didn't like being vulnerable at all.

Heart Memo - The thought of becoming a mother is petrifying; it cracks you wide open in every sense of the word and it does heighten your senses, bringing an entirely new version of the world overnight. But I won't say that you don't know love until you've had children because, quite frankly, that's a shitty thing to say in a world where not everyone can or will have the children they dream of. Love takes many forms, and we do it a disservice by limiting it to motherhood. What I will say, though, is that motherhood is the scariest hood I've ever been in. And I've done some dive bar gigs in my time!

It might come as little surprise that I was one of the lucky ones who did live to see not only one but two children born into the world through my body. This fact still blows my mind today. Even now, as I watch them carve their paths out into the world, I cannot fully grasp that these souls came in through the doorway that is me.

Journal Entry — November 2013

She's here!!! I did it!!

Her tiny little hand wrapped around mine last night, and I think I realised a part of me is not long from now going to be running around on her own. God, that is petrifying.

What if I get it wrong? What if I break her? What if I take her to places where she isn't safe, I'll never forgive myself. What if she grows up to hate me? The collision of thoughts — UGH. She is so adorable: her fiery red hair and curious blue eyes. We created this. Something with so much love and potential. And lungs! She has her mother's lungs, the ward sister said this morning. Ha ha.

Possibly has something to do with the fact she came in at 5 a.m. to tell me and the woman opposite to hush and get some rest. (Water off a duck's back, lady!) I am invincible!

I should probably get some breakfast — I'm sure I can smell toast from the breakfast room.

Also — Eternally grateful to the woman who whispered in the dark that I should take a jug of cold water into the bathroom with me last night. I'm not sure which one in this room it was; it seems strange to ask, "Which one of you saved my vagina from the fiery pits of hell? Can I buy you a large drink?" She will forever be an angel in my eyes.

BREAKFAST IS CALLING! Motherhood begins! Cxx

Motherhood itself comes with a new voice that is often not our own. Society whispers, shouts, and sometimes even demands that we fit into a mould carefully crafted over generations. A good mother is patient. A good mother is selfless. A good mother is always fulfilled by her children alone.

But the reality of motherhood is much more of a mixed bag. Firstly, let's be clear here: not all of us get the mothers we deserve, and secondly, parents are also human, and being human brings an entire treasure trove of emotions and pre-parental trauma to the family table.

I believe one of the biggest errors we make is thinking a 'maiden' vanishes the moment she gives birth, and a mother simply appears. Finding your version of motherhood takes time; and every child, partnership, and household is entirely different. What I wish someone had told me from the start is that it is impossible to be a perfect mum. But being a good mum in the small ways day-to-day — and it might look different over time — but it is possible, even on the days you think you have failed. You just keep trying. I have never known a parent regret trying, but I have known many who deeply regret giving up.

As a mother of course, I immediately rebelled. I didn't have visitors, instead I went to see other people when my children were born. Never is a woman more popular than when she has had a baby, and that is an awful truth.

You suddenly get phone calls from relatives who have never been to your house, and you are expected to hand over your newborn so everyone can sniff and coo over them. The entire thing made me itch at the thought, let alone when standing in a room and letting it happen because it's expected.

I watched my phone ping for hours to arrange visits. Meanwhile I was stuck between the overwhelming influx of love for this redheaded bundle in my arms and the distaste in my mouth that people I hadn't seen or heard from for months wanted to suddenly come over for "baby cuddles" at the earliest convenience. I was about to become a walking mixture of feminine rage and joy; what a hormonal cocktail that would be for the world!

After our first night at home we heard a relatively early morning knock at the front door. I peeped through the bedroom window, wondering who on earth gave this person our address. The dogs barked until they left the front pathway while I was filled with an unexpected rage. Who tracks down someone's address and visits unannounced when that person has just had a baby?

Once I had a rather large and frothy coffee in my hand, I reframed the idea; they were probably just stopping off with a card before work and wouldn't have wanted to come in. I needed to calm myself and understand it was the intention that mattered most; and that is the little nugget I have carried forward with me. Was the issue because these people didn't usually think about us twice? or was the real frustration more that I didn't feel able to tell them where to go?

We spent one day together before Ashley had to return to work curled up in bed as our fresh little bundle snoozed. Together we talked about how we wanted our family to be different and how the things that worked for other people wouldn't work for us. Being super laid back, Ashley agreed with most things I proposed, but didn't want to upset the wider family.

Remember, we were young and less likely to upset the apple cart in those days; I imagine our boundaries would have been even higher if we had done early parenthood in our thirties. No Christmas Day rushing around, no sending birthday cards to kids who don't even know our name. You know, the usual things you get sucked into because that's what it means to be a good parent and a good family member. In later years we've learned that what counts is emotional support and acceptance rather than celebrations and forced photos for social media.

My midwife warned me four days in that she thought I was still running on adrenaline and that, at some point, it would run out – she feared I might hit a wall because I was never home. I reminded her that I thought I was going to die during birth. This wasn't adrenaline; this was the joy of life running through my veins, and I knew not every pregnant woman had this feeling after giving birth, so I was going to let it continue for as long as possible.

She asked me how feeding was going – I had refused to breastfeed. I don't share this with some sort of science to back it up, and this is not a reason for the "breast is best" brigade to come at me, I share it from a place of guilt-free humanness. I wanted my body back. I wanted to wrap myself in the softest cocoon of clothes and simply hold my exhausted self until she or I fully healed.

Finally, after all the checks, she smiled and said: "You were always gonna be a rebel mama." I nodded as she reminded me I had her number if needed.

As I watched her retreat down the garden path I thought about the fact she wasn't entirely wrong. I was born to rebel in many senses of the word, but also I wanted a slow life. I wanted to sing to my baby and tell her the stories I had always craved, the real fairytales where curses weren't always as they seemed. I wondered if such a thing was possible. How could I join the two sides of what I wanted for our life?

THE SONGS THAT SAVED ME

During those early years I spent a lot of time with a baby at home alone, whilst Ashley was working a crazy amount of hours to keep us afloat. As lonely as that was, it gave me time to return to music.

Although it had never really left me — music was in my blood. However the two of us immersed ourselves into song to the point that I dragged my floor-standing mission speakers and a full stack system into the nursery. We danced and played, I talked to her about music, and we napped with my favourite albums on repeat. It is no surprise to me now that my daughter constantly has headphones on for 90% of her day.

I remember as a child sitting in the back of my Dad's burgundy Mondeo listening to the Michael Jackson song *Music and Me* as hot tears ran down my face. As I closed my eyes tightly to block out the rain and let the melody sweep through my body for the last minute. I knew this feeling, I knew this song's truth, because I felt it everyday, and to this day music has held me as if it were my best friend. With no expectations music finds a way of meeting us at every emotion and point of nostalgia.

Music has saved me over and over again. When I feel as if I have sunk too deep for anyone else to meet me, music meets me somehow at the depths with the words and the wisdom I can't seem to find the grace for in the moment.

I'm unsure I can even explain how much music has healed me. This book actually started with a playlist to anchor me into those times of memory; a little musical journey through the past, if you will. And I'll most probably cry through those very same songs as we prepare to hit the day of publication. But during those exhausting and emotional first weeks at home alone, music held us both and I believed my daughter loved it as much as I did.

Music was with me when I sang for the first time at the Karate Christmas Party and music was with me on the stage every single time after. I sometimes think of the eleven-year-old girl, bundle of cash in her back pocket after two 45-minute sets, sitting with a cola and a packet of ready salted crisps and realise that, even then, all those years ago, it was me and the music.

It could be two friends in the car driving on the motorway singing at the top of their lungs, karaoke with friends, an empty pub on a Saturday, Cardiff Millennium Stadium, a local elderly people's home or the Bristol Hippodrome and back; it didn't matter as long as there was me and the music, because music was there every step of the way;.

I did my last paid gig locally two weeks before my daughter's first birthday and haven't sang on your typical stage since. But that doesn't mean I forget music. Each of us has a connection to music, for some it is simply easier to spot. We made mixtapes, burnt CD's, queued up for concert tickets at the box office; we sent playlists to boyfriends and added songs to our social media.

Every time we tap our foot, clap our hands, sing or move our bodies we are moving old energy and calling in the new. I'll never forget standing on the moors last year and watching a group of dowsers measure the width of the ley line there before and after the circle I was part of and sang and danced. The land loves music as much as I do.

Many of us think we need to read music, sing or play an instrument to be connected to music, but this couldn't be further from the truth. Our bodies respond to music, sometimes through the memory of a shared experience, other times through goosebumps on the back of your neck at a concert or the feeling of the bass rippling through your chest.

Whenever I couldn't find the words, she was there with an offering. When I felt as if teenage hormones or rage might take over, there was a burnt CD made by a friend or a record I used to listen to as a child. Music seemed to flood in like water and fill in those holes that life sometimes seems to bore into us.

It's not just me either; we use music to celebrate, to mourn and to bring us together. Music is storytelling at its finest, because it has melody and also because you only have a few minutes to convey the emotion and intention of the song.

By the time I was six years old I knew music would always be my companion. She continued to be there also in the later years when my children were sad, at bathtime, parties, on the radio in the house, or on road trips. We now have family songs that make us all think of the same thing simultaneously.

Music connects us through stories of love, lust, betrayal and mistakes. Sometimes, the song doesn't need words; the melody carries the story all by itself. If the world were a stage, as Shakespeare said, then music is the one thing that has always been there and didn't require me to trust it. It didn't need work like so much of the rest of this story.

Music met me over and over again. People in my life may have come and gone. Music has carried me through every emotion and continues to lift me when I need it with mixtapes for adventures and kitchen discos.

Now, the difference is that my voice was only mine. I sing to the land and to myself, to the future to come and the memories of the past.

After years of using my voice for destruction, I guess what I really wanted was to build something for the future. Something that would still be here when I am long gone, something worth the use of my vocal cords. I just needed to figure out what that was. Singing in that nursery with my daughter in my arms helped me figure out exactly what that might look like.

THE SHIFT FROM EXPECTATION TO REALITY

When my children were still young they both came down with chicken pox. Nights blurred into each other and sleep became a distant memory. One night, with both of them curled up on my lap, I sang them back to sleep by the light of the gas fire a friend had lent us.

Wrapped in extra blankets, I watched a deer move across the field under the Moon, condensation trailing down the window of the mobile home we had somehow ended up in. And in that quiet, exhausted moment, I wondered how something so beautiful could be so profoundly intertwined with something so painful. That feeling right, there is my definition of parenthood in today's world.

Early parenthood is one of a kind. We each have our styles, triggers, and ideal visions of how we want or wish things to be. I always thought I would be the mum with the wooden toys, the beautiful garden, and the immaculate house; I wanted to bake and cook home-cooked meals. Little did I know back then, straight out of the parenting gate, that this was just one of many patriarchal bars for us as women to try and canter over.

We are told that a mother should find joy every moment, yet no one talks about the loneliness that can creep in during midnight feeds or the mental exhaustion of answering a curious toddler's constant "Why?"

We are told that a mother should sacrifice without complaint, but what about the deep longing for personal identity beyond motherhood? I won't recommend you mention that one too loudly at a parent and toddler group, because I did once and I was met with cold stares and less than friendly responses.

During those first few years, we had every challenge thrown at us; from losing jobs to losing homes, and watching friends we thought we would have for life drift away in silence. For a very long time, life felt like unnecessarily hard work. But there was just so much joy, laughter and learning all woven in between those hard times.

Everywhere we look everyone seems to make it look easy. "Five minute clean girl eyeshadow look", which is pretty much makeup to look flawless while still looking like you aren't wearing any makeup!? Pinterest boards on how to do everything, organisers on social media, videos of quick and easy methods for all the things.

But what if it wasn't easy? We could take that a step further and ask - What if it isn't meant to be easy? To begin with I tried to make it all look *easy*. Everywhere we showed up clean, tidy and organised. You want wet wipes I've got them; you want a spare pen and piece of paper, I got you don't worry. The illusion was in making it look effortless. Because that's the point, right? Wrong. What that actually does is set you up for exhaustion and burn out.

We want to appear composed and consistent, giving the impression that everything comes easily and we're fully in control. As the years have gone on I don't tend to do this as much anymore and if you do, please stop. It's creating unrealistic expectations for the outside world and the young mum next door, it's unnecessary stress for us all. Honesty helps us all in the long run.

When we think we have to choose between exhaustion and making it look easy, both options are on the same street to the very same destination: failure. You'll feel like a failure because you are exhausted or you'll feel like a failure because you didn't make it look easy. There are no winners in this.

To override that conditioning you are gonna have to get vulnerable in all the ways; my number one realm of this is in parenting.

I have seen many different types of mothers over the years. The stay-at-home mum whose only focus is her children, to the point that she has holes in her socks and hasn't bought a new bra in six years; the corporate mum who drops her baby off at childcare and cries to the office; the mum who somehow manages to juggle working from home and having children around her feet asking when they can have a snack or go to the park. I have concluded that there is no easy option, it is just a lot of sacrifice for one thing or another.

I considered how much women carried in silence; I couldn't be the only one exhausted. I did an excellent job of pretending I wasn't, but if I were a flamingo, I would have been the pale pinkest of flamboyants.

I grew up in what was often an emotional rollercoaster of a house, where my mother's emotions would usually set the tone for the entire family. Imagine everyone in their own little rowing boats and her emotions as the gnarly tide that would often lead me to feel as if I was sinking. I can't speak for my siblings. This memory led me down a slippery slope of perfectionism as a mother myself. Because if I appeared in control then everyone else was able to carry on.

Looking back I don't remember ever witnessing an apology for an emotional outburst, or a calm explanation after an event from either of my parents. That's a generational thing maybe and I can accept that. Now fourteen years into motherhood I see that as much as we are governed by our emotions and the moon as women, as an adult personally I have found that a quick and heartfelt apology calms the seas rather than everyone trying to pretend it didn't happen.

ack in the early 2000s, I was showing up to all the family things, responding in all the expected ways while running a small business with minimal support – partly because I was a strong, independent woman, and partly because, as we know, firstborns aren't encouraged to ask for help. As my children grew older, I watched my friends – those who became parents later in life move through their own awakening to parenthood. And still, it took years before I began to notice the emerging patterns of exhausted women everywhere.

In all my years, I could not remember witnessing a relaxed woman and I'm not the first to mention this; I have heard Liz Gilbert speak on it many times too. As a child, I saw women dropping kids off at school and running down the pathway to get to work on time; I saw mums prepping lunches and dinners in between ferrying around grandparents to hospital appointments. I never remember seeing a woman sitting in the sun with a book or planning lunch with the girls. Every woman I can remember was exhausted from carrying the silent responsibility of their family. What I didn't know was why?

Why were women running around trying to be all the things; from taxi driver, counsellor to friend, parent, nurse, chef and so much more? Is it any surprise that most women say they feel 'tired' even when they don't have the words to express why the tears are falling? "I'm just tired," we say, but what are we tired of? The long list of silent expectations? The fact that our society uses phrases such as: "Only a housewife", or tells us that we shouldn't want more from life when we have children; we can't have it all, because if we have it all then what happens?!

I didn't want my kids to witness this exhausted woman I had become for a second longer. I was becoming more and more frustrated which is never a good sign. The constant lists, the slamming of cupboard doors, the huffing and puffing when it all got too much. What was this teaching my daughter, who may choose to have her own children? What was this showing my son? Rage-filled me with that realisation that the world was happy to encourage women to be stressed and exhausted juggling everything from Pinterest mum goals to businesses or work and a clean home to match.

One day, when I explained to my husband that exhausted women were fueling the world, he met me with a response that I had not seen coming. He replied to my rage, explaining that many women expect too much and that there is a duality here; we are all missing out because men are exhausted, too. I did my best not to roll my eyes and I listened.

Men are told they must provide and be emotionally available. Still, they must also be the point of safety and protection, so they can't crumble because if they crumble, the family crumbles along with them. They must show up for their families but not be afraid to make time for the gym and their hobbies. Don't we all expect too much? Each wanting to be seen, heard, valued and loved. Had I missed another part of the problem? Were men feeling the same way as women? Was the system they created now becoming a cage?

I believe it was Martha Beck that once said: "Your children will not treat themselves the way you treat them. Your children will treat themselves the way you treat yourself." And for me, this meant I needed my children to see me putting my mental health first rather than giving away everything, being left with nothing physically and energetically. I didn't need to make it look easy or hide my emotions. I simply needed to give myself what I needed.

I began to focus on cyclical living, following not just according to the seasons and my cycles, but also the cycles I could now recognise of our family. We moved to what we call the house on the hill, which was a whole new level of self-discovery. The walls grew mould, our belongings were ruined — the majority destroyed, and we relocated to Yorkshire for a fresh start and a slower pace of life. I didn't push against my intuition like I used to. I harnessed it like a forgotten super power.

In all this business of parenthood I just hadn't noticed that I was slowly and unknowingly evaporating. I'm not talking about keeping up with the latest fashion, regular haircuts, or carving out time for passions; by the time my children were six and four, I had utterly lost so many original and influential parts of myself that I was not sure I knew who I was or who I wanted to be.

Society's idea of motherhood would have us believe we must sacrifice every part of ourselves for our children. Amongst the many voices of society, we often hear those of guilt, self-doubt and comparison. I used to scroll through social media hoping it would help me be like the other mums, but the truth is we are all generally making it up as we go along, and the prettiness of social media is never the real story. I chose to return to many of the things I loved as a child in those little pockets of time, until the children got older and the time slowly increased.

The next penny dropped when we were walking back from the allotment after school one day. I don't remember the exact situation, which is unlike me. However, I remember declaring I was sick of putting out fires for everyone! The arguments, the misunderstanding, and the lack of listening. I was no longer willing to be the communications manager of this family because I was exhausted. My daughter, still dressed as Little Red Riding Hood from World Book Day, looked up at me and said quite simply: "We never asked you to do that, mama."

I whipped my head around to look at my husband in shock and, in his usual cool-as-a-cucumber demeanor, he nodded knowingly and said: "She's got a point, babe." So, at that moment, we agreed I was no longer going to be the go-between and recognised that, for a while, that might not be fun for everyone.

Journal entry that night:

Have I been forcing everyone to get along? Have I been over parenting? Finding solutions rather than letting them figure it out for themselves? Today I wondered all of this with my hands in the dirt. We've decided that I should try and let everyone sort out their own misunderstandings. No more explaining what one or the other missed. No more buffering and, if I am honest, I feel sick at the thought. The tears this is going to cause. I've spent so long running this household, I am so used to having things in a routine, I'm not sure what will happen when I let go of the wheel a little, but I guess we will see.

All I can do is trust. I have seen too many families fall apart due to lack of communication. Perhaps letting them figure it out will open new pathways of communication for the people I love? Reckon I'll gain a few more scars on my tongue as I adjust to this! Cxx

For me to be able to step back though, we all needed to learn how to communicate in ways that worked for us, not only as a family unit but also in pairs and small groups. The way I communicate with my daughter isn't the same as how her younger brother or even my husband does. We all needed to strengthen our communications individually as well as collectively and, what's more, we needed to honour our voices as a team and individually.

This was one of the hardest things I have ever watched in our household. I was at home most of the time for years, while Ashley worked long hours and spent nights away from home, but was now in a new job and home every evening.

During the first few weeks of this attempt to let them figure it out for themselves, I'm sure I got scars on my tongue from the amount of biting I did. I'd watch them navigate their misunderstandings with an unstoppable itch to jump in and smooth things over. This made me realise how alert I was of my surroundings and everyone's interactions, whereas if I wasn't talking to Ashley or my kids directly, they weren't listening.

I saw how their awkward conversations about how many toys they could take in the car or why Daddy was tired and a little grumpy brought them closer together and gave them a better understanding of each other. I watched as they compromised on what they each wanted and needed. Even if it was five minutes more time to watch a programme or finish a game.

All this time I thought speaking for them was helping and, quite possibly, it was preventing them from this deep connection I wanted, and they wanted all along. Now I look back and realise that if one of us is away or out of the house, I know that everyone can communicate clearly. Rather than one of us carrying it all on our shoulders. It was a hard pill to swallow standing on the football field that day, but I am grateful that my child could speak her wisdom without fear of judgment.

I had always prided myself on my awareness of what my children were witnessing and how they were always watching, yet I hadn't always fully taken an extra moment to understand the importance of what they were saying. Did I hear them? Of course, but was I listening deeply? That was the next question to tackle, because parenthood is a constant evolution.

Sometimes the only thing you can do is remind yourself, in that very moment, that you've never parented a child at this age before, and you've never been the parent you are right now. Quite often, we all need to give ourselves a little grace and understand mistakes and misunderstandings will always happen. That is just a part of life.

THE FREEDOM OF BEING MISREAD

I grew up in the era of pagers, which slowly gave way to mobile phones with the game Snake on them, followed by ringtones of your favourite song that you paid to download. The closest thing we had to behind-the-scenes stories was MTV Cribs. And before Facebook poking there was Myspace, and before Starlink there was dial-up.

In today's world we have access to external voices constantly. We have social media, voice notes, constant news channels and podcasts all sharing people's thoughts, ideas and experiences. It can feel a little overwhelming at times, as if we are not only saturated but obsessed with being heard, even worse on the days when it feels as if everyone is shouting.

This is one of the reasons I personally stopped watching the news back when my children were young. Let's skip over the propaganda for a minute and also the thoughts of my self-ignorance. I prefer to call it self-preservation. You see, it hurts my heart.

I realised that the news wasn't actually helping me with anything, it just left me feeling disappointed with the world, angry at the current global leadership, fed the fears within and, to be quite honest, it distracted my thought pattern, which left less time for the things I wanted to do and more time for me to slip into a downward spiral of how awful the world is and quite often tearful before bed.

I decided it was best for me to go back to how it was many years ago, when we only knew the news of our village. I needed to trust that not only was I safe, even though the man on the television hadn't told me so today, but also that if something was truly important, someone would tell me about it. My mind got dramatically quieter the night I stopped watching the news and picked up a book instead.

I often wonder how off balance the voice of our media is knowledge is power of course, but when does it become a force feeding daily frenzy of fear and worry before we all go to sleep? I wonder how many millions of homes watch the ten o'clock news only to find themselves consumed with rage or trying to pick a murderer in their mind as they fall asleep. I don't think I have the answers but I do know that, for me, if it's important for my safety someone will tell me; it will be global or someone that knows me well will know I will need to hear it.

Social media has created a false sense of relationship and entitlement. "If you post, I have the right to comment, critique, and demand more," and that's even deeper an issue when the audience assumes emotional access to someone they don't actually know. This voice overload comes with several rather blurry lines we seem to be crossing.

Firstly, we assume that we are entitled to access to people. We see it with celebrities, but it also happens with professionals, family, and friends. The boundary between public and private has all but vanished and the world is almost encouraging this. The expectation that everyone must be available all the time, has become the norm, and it's not only exhausting but it often means the quality in which we share is often '*lacking*'.

People have the right to be heard; that I do not disagree with. The issue is that because there are now spaces provided for them to speak, some believe they have a right to an audience. And that access to an audience leads people to wrongly believe they are entitled to say whatever they want, whether it be offensive or not.

Then there is the issue that just because someone has a platform it doesn't mean their voice is well informed, or with an intention of contributing to a world for the better. We often confuse presence with substance and that can be dangerous. But the solution isn't as simple as silence, it is about being held accountable.

In a nutshell big enough that humanity could quite possibly choke on it, there is a great deal of entitlement and expectation around the voices we hear in the world today where we mistake "freedom of speech" for "freedom from consequence.

I'm a truthseeker. Always have been, it's why I research, how I find myself in the deepest of rabbit holes and often why I ask questions. Most recently, due to the use of AI I have found myself doubling down on written content on paper, I find myself squinting at screens to see if the words someone is apparently speaking match the shapes their mouths are making, I count fingers in images and check comments to see if anyone knows if a video is true.

We now live in a world where voices are not just spoken or written — they are manufactured, cloned, and sold back to us. Marketing no longer only sells us products; it sells us people's identities, beliefs, even their humanity. With AI, a voice doesn't even need to belong to a real person anymore. It can be shaped, remoulded, and used to persuade, distract, or consume.

The danger is that this creates a double distortion. Not only do we doubt whether *their* voice is real, but we begin to doubt whether *ours* is. When algorithms echo back to us what we want to hear, when AI mimics our tone, when marketing tells us what we should want before we even ask for it — our voice becomes harder to locate.

What we need is to cultivate our own individual discernment; we need to stop shouting, and we need to forgive our mistakes and choose to do better. It's a journey of a thousand steps, but I do believe it can be done.

In a world of misinformation and shouting its beginning to get even louder and it often takes the brunt of the blame. But what about those much quieter external voices? Once we continue to hear and more often than not believe and claim as our own?

Heart thread — In a world where our voices are constantly being misshapen by the media, by marketing, by AI, and by our own misconceptions; our task is not to silence ourselves, but to return to the root of our voice. To find the place within us that cannot be cloned, sold, or drowned out. Because when we speak from that quiet, rooted centre, our voices are no longer tangled in misconception — they become threads of truth, clarity, and connection.

THE TINY SOULS WHO TAUGHT ME TO LISTEN

A younger voice is often ignored or considered to have the least value around the table. This ties in with the idea that only with age comes wisdom. What if we are, in fact, born with all the wisdom and our years only allow us to remember it. If we could listen to children a little more rather than talking over them and thinking we know better than them on all things, we might not only learn something, but we might also prevent our children from a longer journey of remembering their own wisdom.

Many would also have us believe that our children's voices hold no wisdom and that what they want or need doesn't matter in the bigger picture of the adult world. But our children's voices shape parenthood, too. Children might have small voices, but that doesn't mean they can't carry big truths; and those truths are often simple and still profound.

Is it because they are said before the world tells them no? Maybe that's true, but as I sat with this when my children were young, I wondered how our children's questions, emotions and needs guide us and how, if we slowed down just a little, we might notice we are being reminded to reflect, tune into the basics of our bodies, and see the world differently through the hearts of our children.

I had always taken the time to listen to my kids, I had acknowledged their emotions and responded the best way I knew how, and even on some level, I knew they were teaching me as much as I was teaching them. But now we were adding a realness to their lessons through their voice day to day. I couldn't help but wonder how different this was from the early days of my childhood; maybe some things we aren't supposed to remember.

To begin with, I was almost parenting them the way I'd wanted to be parented, only to realise that wasn't entirely what they needed at all; they needed to be supported in very individual ways, beyond any parenting book I had read so far. We had family meetings disguised as picnics or breakfasts in bed, and my researcher brain took votes.

We asked each other what we needed or wanted from the weekend. Ashley and I wanted them to know their voices mattered, even at four years old, when they didn't want to leave the house because they wanted to pretend they were a cat named Trevor who slept on the end of a bed all day. We encouraged them to share what they desired and then sometimes meet us halfway with a compromise; we still do this now, only across the breakfast table or at the end of the day.

Of course, with age comes wisdom. But does that mean we should crush younger voices or gatekeep our experience from them? Not in my world, and for me the best place to start this was within our own home. It's been a journey of rediscovering the delicate balance between giving my kids the space to express themselves and showing them that what I need as a woman is at least equally important as my role as a mother. This also goes for their father and his needs.

We hadn't been used to our family's voices before. I suppose when the children were so young, many decisions were made while they were in bed. But once we invited them to the table, I wanted them to feel the weight of decisions — intellectually, physically, emotionally and spiritually. I wanted them to learn how things felt in their bodies and to be able to share that when we made decisions. Because as adults I wouldn't be there to prompt this connection of depth of process.

So we made it a practice, and still do, to give them a few days to think about a potential holiday booking or plans for guests visiting. It's not just about making the right decision, it's about learning to sit with the options, feel into them, and then share their thoughts.

I hope to run our household as a team with basic ground-level equal rights, no matter each person's age or gender. And as a mother, I want to see my children create similar things in their own homes in the future or, better still, new ways that work for them.

Just when I thought I had mastered this balance, a crucial realisation came when my daughter was seven years old and was signed off on the last week of school with exhaustion. I looked at her purple-circled eyes as she tried to eat a sandwich at the table, her mouth full of ulcers. I wondered if I should have made her soup to go with that sandwich, damn it! It was another failure to add to the list.

I watched her heavy eyes and wondered where the spark had gone. Later that afternoon, we picked her brother up from nursery and he clung to me, sinking his head into my neck and squeezing me tightly. We walked back home across the frosty train tracks to the warmth of the house where we snuggled on the sofa with hot Vimto and a biscuit, waiting for Ashley to get home from work for tea.

A character on the TV declared, "I'm so very, very tired." "Me too," said Bella from the left. I looked down at her and pulled her in a little closer. Before I could respond, Theo said, "I am so tired as well." I squeezed them both, and my mind drifted from the TV to wonder how long we had all felt exhausted. For me, the exhausted mother pattern in our home has been present possibly since around 2010. When people told me to "Get your sleep while you can!" Little did I realise that the little people in our household also carried this tiredness.

I realised it wasn't the children pushing for more, it was the adults. No, it was society. I mentally ran through what I call 'the family bloopers reel'.

Bella had decided to smudge a family friend with some incense at four years old. She entered the kitchen while I made our guests a cup of tea and asked for incense. I thought her father had sent her; it wasn't until I walked into the snug with the tray that I saw her clearing one of our guests' energy fields, eyes closed, Sun on her face. The embarrassment of it, even as a memory! Until I let my human emotions settle and reminded myself she wasn't wrong! This person did tend to have a rather pessimistic view of life and seemed to feel most comfortable in conversations that were more moaning or complaining than anything else.

I watched my son catch crumbs from his 4 p.m. snack in his lap and remembered all the times I would say, "So sorry we are late," only for him to follow up with "We didn't want to come," or "We wanted to stay in the warm." This is one of the reasons I stopped apologising for being late and replaced the phrase with: "Thanks for waiting for us."

Our children don't have society's filters placed on them, so they tend to express exactly how they feel. They might yell, "HAPPY!! " in celebration if they play with their toys. In the same way, they will openly cry or tell you when they are sad or tired. My children also have a knack for calling people out on their lies. I wonder where they get that from...

Children aren't afraid to ask questions either. How does that work? Why does it only grow here? What are you doing, Mama? Why do you do it that way, Daddy?

They aren't afraid to ask questions, but it's more than that; they also aren't afraid to get things wrong, to try something with zero fear of being judged.

Right then, I knew this path wasn't working for any of us. The greatest lie we have been sold is that we must look to others for direction. However I knew we needed to simplify our household; not in the traditional sense of the word, but in an ancient sense. So we decided to follow our own intuition and home-educate, which remains one of the biggest and best decisions we have ever made.

For the first time, I put my family above everything else. Their needs exceeded the school requirements, and invitations to parties that would most probably be extremely noisy. Our needs as a unit became my focus.

People's true colours show when you start to put your own needs first, and I saw some things I didn't expect, including some hard truths about relationships and expectations from others. Yet something inside me had broken when the female line of my family banished me from my immediate bloodline (we'll get to that story later!). It had been a turning point, if you will; a separation that allowed me to carve my path and find my voice.

If life were a blackboard, we would dust it off and start again with a new plan; one where we were the important ones. Instead of running around serving others first and putting ourselves last, we would become the priority. For me, doing that felt foreign at first; wrong in a way, but it was the first step toward freedom.

We started our early tradition of vision boards. It was simple: we would create a vision for the upcoming year or season. This gave us a chance to see, as a family, what everyone was heading towards, and it created a collective sense of direction. I had spent so much time creating new ways for them to share their dreams and ideas; part of my intention was to raise children who understood that their desires were necessary, that their voices had power, and that possibility was always within reach.

We encouraged our kids to continue to ask questions. We began telling them why we made certain decisions and how we happened to understand our errors. We have even been known to discuss other people's behaviour on the way home in the car from visits or parties because there are always examples for us to grow, learn, and be inspired by. As they got older, I encouraged them to question everything, including their ability to ask me. Well, let me tell you that it took some getting used to!

Let me be clear here: this is not a judgment for judgment's sake. It doesn't make us feel any better or inflate our egos. It helps me share with my children the patterns of why someone might, I don't know, shout at their partner or constantly belittle other people in the room. It's a lesson on how differently we can choose to behave which I hope carries them through into adulthood so they can lead their lives aware of what they are putting out into the world, whilst also having discernment of others and keeping a firm idea of the person they want to be.

Now, we aren't perfect. Occasionally, we still have to call out miscommunication; we wouldn't be having a human experience if we didn't. My husband is an incredible father, but if you aren't talking directly to him, you can usually bet he isn't listening. He also has no constant inner dialogue, so let's be clear here, his brain does not work like mine does.

On the other hand, my daughter is super independent, and I often forget to ask if she wants me to listen or give her suggestions for a solution. My son likes to internally process things before he shares, so you cannot force him to talk things through until he is ready. And all of this can and will change as we each move along our paths. We only know this because we constantly keep the communication lines open.

They were raised equally on honesty and banter. We have quick tongues in this house, but we are equally as fast to apologise if something has upset someone else.

They seem to need me less recently and that makes me a little sad. OK, that is a lie; it makes me ache a little at times. It feels as if they now have a piece of my heart, and they get to run around and make decisions about how and what they do with it. And yet some wise ancient part of me knows this is a part of the process.

As they become teenagers I have to regularly remind myself that it isn't my job to protect them anymore, the same way it wasn't my job to do everything for them or buffer life's ups and downs once they reached a certain age, not in the ways I used to when they were babies. Watching your children find their own voice can be brutal at times to witness. You see them navigate friendships and yes, make silent judgements on their friendship choices. But my job now is to trust them as individuals to make the best choices for them, and learn from the times that maybe they didn't.

We are still working on this, though, and I can't say I have mastered it, but I can say that I wish someone had told me that my voice, my ideas, and the way I choose to raise my children are not wrong. Family is not about fitting into a mould, it is about creating our oath as a branch of an even bigger family tree that feels authentic and sustainable and, most importantly, honours all of the voices within that family unit.

I vowed to communicate my thoughts more clearly. It started with being honest about my emotions when I was tired or apologising when I responded when engulfed in emotion until taking a beat. As my children have gotten older, I now share the intrusive words that go through my mind, the thoughts that we usually keep to whispers, because I want to normalise them. Normalising is how we shift from shame to connection.

In our house, we normalise human behaviour: no unnecessary masking, all the talking. If they ask me what I'm thinking, I tell them. If we leave a place and I am concerned about some behaviour they witnessed, I won't sit in the silence and shame of having put them in that situation; I'll share it.

Note here: sharing is not projecting – there is a big difference. I share my feelings about what we witnessed and ask them if they want to share theirs.

Does this always work? No. But does it help them to see that their feelings of shame and their emotions are normal? Yes. And if that is one of the gifts I can give them, I will return to the ocean as a happy mermaid at the end of this life.

I want them to always be able to return to their own voice with ease. Too often, our voices are handed over to the outside world, or we are told we must label them in a fixed way. In reality, our voices are constantly shifting – influenced by social media, friends, and groups outside of ourselves. If we're not careful, we start speaking with other people's voices, and our own become harder to recognise.

The voices that once felt so chaotic – the children's voices and my own – became clearer. Our voices. We started to hear each other more deeply, more intentionally. And perhaps the most powerful voice of all was the one inside me, the one I had silenced for so long. But now, I let it speak. It had a lot to say.

Life became less about noise and more about truth, less about fulfilling expectations and more about honouring our shared possibilities. And that's when I realised that the voice of possibility is not a how-to guide, it's not about following a prescribed formula or method. It's about discovering your path and voice and understanding that the journey is less about finding the answers and more about embracing the questions.

In those moments of pause, of listening – not just to others, but to yourself – possibility begins to unfold. It's more about being heard than even validation. Confirm that you have listened to your child or your partner. Repeat what they have said back to them if needed. I say this because even though I am now an adult and a parent, I can still have a sharp tongue that often speaks before my brain can catch up.

My current challenge - My daughter reminds me daily that she isn't asking me for a solution. She simply wants to share or express what she is experiencing. That's my personal work in progress because I figured that out in friendships; however, as a parent, it somehow feels harder not to continually give the practical solution. Parenting is a continuous spiral like all of life. Everything is changing and never perfect. So don't go believing I have it all mastered.

What was my biggest lesson in those early parenting years? I've never been one to bypass anything. I might spit my dummy out and stamp my feet occasionally, but I won't back down from an opportunity to grow.

In fact, I have even been known to root around looking for things I can work on. However, what I hadn't seen coming was the constant droplets of me bypassing my joy. I love my children unconditionally. But somehow the world is telling mothers to bypass our joy for eighteen years or more and I'm not quite sure that is correct or for the best.

It takes balance to be a mother and to also not avoid your joy at the same time. And it's not one of those fifty-fifty things either. Sometimes it's a ten minute walk or singing your voice out as you cook tea to songs you like that aren't from a children's movie. OK sometimes those are my favourite too, but you get the point!

There are so many lessons that rise from parenting, and my most recent one is simple yet profound: the power of joy — is for everyone. All of us. As a family, we each need to return to supporting every member in finding that.

I speak from the belly, not the script.
I speak from the mothers who never had time to speak.
I speak from the street corners and kitchen sinks.
I speak from the ache, from the ancestor, from the ash.
I speak from the wild, the worn, the waiting.
I speak from the soul's memory.
And I speak now –
Not because I'm ready.
But because the silence is too heavy to carry alone.

THE STRENGTH OF WEARY WOMEN

We all need to stop pretending we are strong. "Fake it until you make it" doesn't work anymore. The same way pretending it is easy. Well it never really worked. But still, this idea that we must have it all together is setting us up to fail. I was pretending during college, and somehow I seemed to be back at a similar phase during motherhood.

We know we can do hard things; of course this is true, but the mistake we make is pretending that those things are easy. It doesn't matter if it's in a work environment or a friendship, we must show up as we are and share from a place that is deeper than "#authentic".

And when we do that in our households, we end up with mental or physical health issues. Spending so long 'holding it together' that the lid pops off and our brain begins a downward spiral., or that our body decides it cannot continue and forces us to stop.

This false sense of rebellion is an epidemic. And it doesn't only happen to women; it happens to everyone. Men are only now being able to share their emotions due to this false narrative around what it means to be the head of a family. All because we would quite literally medicate or die than be seen as vulnerable or, the worst, weak.

Rather than change the system, we find it easier to silence our bodies with medication so we can 'soldier on'. This phrase blows my mind, because do you know the one thing the military does better than anything? It crushes you, removes your identity and disconnects you from your emotions. Yes, the lingo and the procedure might have more red tape and rules now, but the roots of it are the same in my eyes. We believe we are in a world of kill or be killed. Guess what? We aren't soldiers and war is rarely for the right reasons. It's more than often about greed.

So what do we have? Women functioning as worker bees, and men in the corporate world believing they are at war. Both exhausted, bone tired, but no one believes they can say so. Because the voice of this modern and mostly wasteland of a world has told us that to not be able to cope with the everyday is a failure.

We convince ourselves of just one more goal, and do one more thing... just wait five more years... But guess what? Five more years is not guaranteed for anyone. Yet we forget this; we forget time is the most precious currency and we tune our brains to listen to the humdrum of society, work until retirement, *then* we can have the life we deserve.

Do you see how backwards that is? Do you see that the world was not created — Gaia was not created — for us to work ourselves to the bone for us to take a two week holiday as a reward each year? I'm here to say: No more. Because is it working for anyone? Is it really working for a single soul on this planet? Not one I know or have read about.

The idea that it is compulsory to be strong is breaking us. Because to be a sacred rebel, to lead in this sacred rebellion that the world needs, we need vulnerability and transparency. And if that feels scary, as if you are standing on the threshold of the uncomfortable and what it means to be human, then that's perfect. That is exactly where we need to be.

The thing is about strength is we so often take it to mean we are doing things without the voice of fear in our ear. Wrong. The voice of fear is always going to be there; true strength is when we acknowledge the words of fear and do it anyway.

THE ROLES THAT KEEP US SAFE

Journal Entry, Spring 2021

This weekend I went through my old journals, mixtapes and playlists, the clippings from newspapers, agency paperwork from showcases and old setlists I'd pulled from the stage before we would leave.

So many characters I had played over the years, roles and masks I had tried out at all ages. There were a lot. Some for protection, others to entertain and a lot of them because these were the roles the world told me I should want to play. I sat and cried at the edge of the river because each of them played a vital role in who I am today.

Sometimes I was the villain, other times the picture of the situation is entirely different now as an adult. I saw the pages as a young adult striking out on my own to what I believed was a 'hero on a quest' like Jack climbing the beanstalk to fight the giants of the corporate world. I saw the mentor figures I had through my life in different jobs and communities fall from grace onto the page, I read my wisdom and my anger amongst many pages of hope as a teen that a fairy godmother or wizard might scoop me up and remind me it was all going to be OK.

I've played all the characters in my life, in many stories across the world. In fact I'm pretty sure people tell stories about me that I have long forgotten. And of course there will be people who have stories about me that I would rather forget

But could I love each of these characters? Forgive them when they did things in moments of rage. Why would I forgive myself? I have done bad things, made wrong turns, burned bridges, taken things that weren't mine, spoken to people with very little empathy. Maybe I could if I remind myself that every mistake has taken me to a deeper version of myself.

Maybe I found this box this week because I've done my time with the roles I have played now in all the phases on all of the stages? That thought feels not only peaceful but a little dangerous.

Once we see every action we make as part of a story, we begin to play a little differently. We become a little braver, stronger, the courage rises from within. I saw a quote this week that said: "If you know what you want to be, then you inevitably become it. That is your punishment, but if you never know, then you can be anything." — Oscar Wilde

There is truth in that. And it's a truth I wish I had known long ago. Because in a world full of labels, going through these boxes has reminded me that all I wanted to be was myself.

If we create from the point of two things meeting, sometimes that's a meeting point where two emotions rub up against each other. Often it is in the grey area of the unknown where logic and intuition meet, yet it always begins inside of us. My favourite things are created this way.

Cx

If this is true then we can also be two things at once right? Constantly being in the process of becoming and feeling OK with creating and sharing from that space. Does it ever end, spirit?

"There is this common misconception that we have a final destination to arrive at. A place of divine knowing, of completeness. It is a conclusion with many names. Separate parts of you can exist within you at the same time, combined they make you whole."

I pondered the words of confirmation on the page. I was never simply a rebel or a good girl. I simply needed to swing the pendulum far and wide to discover I could be both at the same time and that I could feel comfortable being both if I stuck with it for long enough.

There is little difference between the spark that starts a revolution and the fire that burns everything down — devotion and rebellion are made of the same flame. The part I had found now in my journals was a reminder that to hold the two was to be my fullest self.

Heart Memo — We all play different characters in life by adapting ourselves to the roles expected of us in different situations: Child, friend, parent, student, lover, leader, and so on. These roles are often unconscious. Sometimes shaped by cultural expectations, personal values, and often survival instincts. Much like actors in a play, we shift tone, behavior depending on the situation. We can become chameleons. This isn't necessarily inauthentic — it's a navigation tool that we can learn from.

THE WORDS LEFT UNSAID

The voice of men is complex, and I haven't always done my best to understand it. If I had, this chapter might have come earlier in the book. When I had my son and witnessed my husband's journey with his voice, it became even more apparent that this was also a part of my journey — to understand men's struggles and complexities. I might not have been born a man, but I have lived and worked alongside them, which made me think I knew them, right? Wrong.

Let me give you an example. One summer, my son was playing with a toy at the park when a child he knew from school came up and yanked it from his hands. Being my son, he refused to let go, and they went back and forth for a few seconds before I stepped in to help them resolve the situation. I took the toy to get their attention and calmly explained that we don't use our bodies to take what we want. I handed it back to my son, and off he went. The other boy's father laughed in my direction and said, "I would have just let them fight it out."

Every cell in my body wanted to snap back with: "I know, and it shows." But I held my tongue. Even though I understood that this was probably part of his upbringing — that he likely knew no better, I was exhausted by the mansplaining in the world. I had reached a point where I shut it down instantly, convinced I was doing it for my children's future.

As a woman, I wasn't fully aware of the extent of this until after I married and had children. Rewind a little and I remember a week before Christmas; I stood opposite Arnos Vale cemetery waiting to get my first tattoo in memory of my friend who had passed away earlier in the year. Snow was on the ground, and the studio shutters were still down.

Checking my phone, I found a message from the tattooist telling me her train was late, but she was on her way. I knew if I left that spot, I wouldn't return through nerves; if I did, it would have to be in the new year. So I waited, huddled against the shutter on the doorstep in an attempt to stop the snow from messing up my hair.

After about forty minutes of waiting, a man came out of the taxi place a few doors up, casually strolled up and asked if I would like a hot drink. I was unsure if this was a safe thing to accept, but he must have sensed the hesitation in my rather expressive face and added, "It won't be anything fancy, but it might warm you up?"

Looking at my slightly blue fingers, I said I would love a tea or a hot chocolate if they had any. Two minutes later, he returned with a brown plastic cup of muddy-looking water. Never have my hands been so pleased with the burning of a flimsy plastic cup! He double-checked that someone was opening up soon. I explained if I left now, I would probably chicken out, and he smiled and said, "Nah, a proper bird like you, you'll be fine". I thanked him again as he went back to the cabby office.

Twenty minutes later, the tattoo studio team arrived with their apologies and unlocked the studio. By the time I had got my coat off and climbed on the couch, a dad and his son had entered, laughing and joking. They asked if this was my first tattoo. I nodded as the reality of why I was here sunk in. I told them it was in memory of my friend, who was a bit of a social butterfly.

As they placed the stencil paper on my neck, the father said, "Oh, ouch! On your neck as well!! That's going to hurt. Probably better off doing it somewhere fleshy." It wasn't what he was saying but more the way he was saying it. I didn't respond as his son joined in the sniggering. "Are you sure you can handle it?" He asked me as the tattooist slid round to face me dead in the eyes and whispered: "I know you can handle this, no show this prick what you are made of." At that moment, a friendship was unlocked. She was right, and I would show him. Georgia and I still laugh about this pillock now.

Forty-five minutes later, I walked through the snow, high on adrenaline, wondering how men were so different. Was it age? Was it a drive to prove themselves? Did they need to always feel in control? Not all men, I thought. Today, a man had seen a stranger on the street in the snow and thought to bring her a hot drink. Two opposite ends of the scale shown to me in less than an hour.

My husband and I had spent countless hours working to understand each other at home. I had learned (and often forgotten) that when he responds with logic, he isn't trying to diminish my emotions; he's simply hardwired to provide solutions. And just as often as I forget that, he forgets that I don't need a logical fix most of the time; I just need to be heard. I believed we had done the work and truly learned to listen to each other. I hadn't entirely managed to extend that understanding into the world.

Around this time, my husband became an advocate for men's mental health, facilitating local meetings and training as a mental health first aider at work. On the outside, I was supportive and encouraging, knowing how needed it was in today's world. But on the inside? I was rolling my eyes. I felt an inner friction that I wasn't proud of.

Did I see the need for men to have a space to offload, share, and learn how to communicate in ways that history had long denied them? Yes, absolutely. But at the same time, we were in the middle of a long-overdue Me Too movement, and what I felt in my bones was that women had been suppressed for thousands of years. And now men were suffering under the very systems they had created.

Yet I couldn't ignore the truth; that my father, husband, or son did not build these structures. They were simply born into them, just as their grandfathers had been before them.

This led to many heated debates in our home, especially when rage burned me from the inside out like cigarette embers. When I'm deep in my emotions, I do not communicate well. There are tears, snot, and words that are sometimes sharper than necessary.

It's not often, but when it happens it feels as if I'm six years old again and all the grace and calmness has been sucked out of the room. I needed to understand why I felt this way. Why was I so triggered? As with most deep-seated emotions and triggers, the answer lay in my past.

I knew my history: The sturdy wall of protection I built when my father left our family home gave me an edge as a young girl. It kept me safe in some ways and allowed me to observe more clearly than most. I grew up in environments where men often surrounded me.

As a teenager, I spent time in pubs and clubs, watching intoxicated men and studying their behaviours. Being in bands as a young woman alongside grown men gave me insights that many my age didn't have. I witnessed personalities clash, saw how they expressed platonic love differently and learned to navigate those dynamics.

I have primarily worked in male-dominated industries — structural engineering companies, car repair centres, and dental practice —-and these experiences shaped me. I love men. I can give as good as I get when it comes to banter, and I will forever be grateful for the men who stepped in and filled different roles after my father left.

I knew good men as well, so why the heck was I so damn angry? I wanted to get to the bottom of it because I was not taking that rage with me into the next phase of life. I have known too many women not to sit with their rage over the years only to find it unavoidable when menopause hits. Was it social media fueling my emotions? Was it something I just needed to sit with and see from both sides?

Still, I spent months in a state of inner turmoil. I didn't want to feel this way. I didn't want to resent men for suddenly seeing themselves as fragile. But at the same time, I also needed them to take responsibility for the fact that one in four women experiences domestic abuse. I knew how little it took for a woman to become unsafe in her own home.

One part of me wanted men to understand that they would never be free until they each took responsibility for their place in history, no matter how big or small. Another part of me wanted to touch foreheads with each of them and remind them that the fight was over. That it's time to communicate in other ways that don't rely on fists, weapons, or bank balances. And another part of me wanted to remind women that we don't need to go to war when the men stop fighting.

It wasn't until a conversation with my husband one evening that something shifted in me. I asked him why he felt so passionate about men's mental health, and he said, "Because I know what it's like to struggle in silence." He spoke about how men, from boyhood, are taught to suppress rather than express themselves and how that conditioning follows them into adulthood. That was the moment I realised my frustration wasn't just with men, it was with a broken system that had silenced all of us in different ways.

Reminding myself of those two kids at school reminds me that both have tiny, tender hearts to protect. On the days when I'm exhausted, when his logic feels like it's suffocating the magic I'm trying to explain or when we rush past each other like ships in the night, I have to tell myself that men and women are not competing. We are not enemies. We are simply two people still figuring it out, always moving forward together.

I have met great men over the years. Solid and reliable, yet self-aware enough to allow themselves to be seen in their softness. They do exist, and

I think it's important to remember that. In the same way, I have also known men who don't understand that no is a complete sentence; I've been followed down alleys, manhandled in nightclubs and pinned up against a kitchen wall by an ex-boyfriend. But I choose not to hate men, and this takes time.

It has taken me years to understand that most of us have never heard the authentic voice of men. That voice should not be mistaken for the version we often hear, it isn't the same. We hear an echo of it distorted by our world, but the authentic voice of men? That needs a place at every table, home, and every heart. That means they must reconnect with their emotions and not be shamed for it as we have been for centuries.

This was a few years ago and is still a work in progress. We talk now and I still have to rein in my inner feminist enough to listen genuinely. The truth is we all see each other through the tinted lenses of our own lives.

The moment we understand that women were not the only casualties of the patriarchy – they were the first but not the only – is the moment the game changes. We can't hate men and simultaneously be a key part of the change. It won't work, because to change the world for the better, as tacky as that might sound, it needs us all.

The first key for me was to remind myself of two things constantly. One: Most men's voices we hear today are not the authentic voice of masculinity. And two: women's voices are woven into stories and intuition, while men's voices are rooted in skills and, more often than not, logic.

My husband isn't applying logic to my emotions because he doesn't believe me, it's just where his magick currently is. They are different, yet both want the same outcome: Unity. I hope we can return to a world where women compete less and share skills more often, and men begin to tell stories as they once did from the heart.

Many notable men have magically made their way into my life: Paul Nicholas, Kim Bloor, Kevin Downes, Alf Cole, Kai Dawe, Pete Willey, Louis Kawolski and, of course, my number one: Ashley Edwards; all teaching me that men can be loving, kind, protective, safe, and reliable in many different ways. Then there are the men in the making, for Theodore Edwards, I can only hope the world sees its way and that your authentic voice is held more tenderly in the future, not just for you but for all men.

Not everyone would choose the bear over a man. There are many safe men in the world; it just feels like it takes a while to find them. They aren't always allowed to speak. Men may not be as silenced as women, but not often enough are men offered a space to simply be themselves, except usually in their own home. Which, when you think of it, is heartbreaking that men are raised to not show even the slightest weakness outside of their own four walls.

At the heart of the voice of the masculine is a need to rewrite the rules of strength, success, and love. We need to remember that love isn't shown through material purchases. It isn't even demonstrated by being the breadwinner or providing a roof over our heads. It is shown in so many other ways that we rarely talk about.

One recent winter weekend, I sat around the kitchen table with two generations of my favourite men. I watched them talk about cars, work, and computer games, each with their passions and drives for the year ahead. And I suddenly realised that not everyone gets to witness this side of the masculine. Some have only seen the darker side of masculinity or been told about it over and over to keep them safe.

And yet, here I was on that day — book on lap, full stomach, even fuller heart — watching my husband load the dishwasher while one of my oldest friends pulled cards and played with the kitchen pendulum. My son sat nearby, devouring an enormous bowl of leftover Yorkshire puddings. And I saw it: the authentic voice of men isn't lost, it may be forgotten by many, but not by all.

We are all trying to figure it out, and that balance is an individual dance that extends beyond our hearts and homes. It ripples into our workplaces, our communities, and our circles. I look around the world today and see us becoming more divided, moving further apart, until we eventually reverse course and come back to see ourselves as one.

Do women hate men? Not at all. We are simply scared of not feeling safe in a world run mainly by men. And how do we change that? I mean, there are so many ways, but for me curiosity is what I would describe as a gateway emotion. I encourage everyone to become more curious for many reasons, but most importantly because hate often comes from a lack of awareness and understanding. We cannot move through it without asking questions. It has been said that fear is a lack of knowing.

Of course, we need to hold men accountable. That includes men calling out their friends and family for inappropriate behaviour. But we also need to remember that it isn't every man. Some days that is harder than others, but then I watch my son and how he cares for those around him and I hope for our future.

Through hate, we must step through the portal of curiosity. Ask more questions. Have difficult conversations. Encourage men in different ways than we encourage women. And we must promote them more often because good men walk this earth, and they need us to remember that.

Heart Thread — We can't focus on the world as it is and simply hope it changes. We have to focus on the world as we want it to be. Our relationships or patterns about how we talk about men is no different. Not out of ignorance, but out of a belief that together we are stronger.

THE PATTERNS OF STORIES AND SKILLS

Standing at the kitchen window, my husband watched our neighbour yet again moving between his van and the garage. "He's always out there, every weekend, isn't he?" he remarked.

I glanced up from the familiar yellow bench at the opposite end of the kitchen. "Yup, he's of that generation, I guess." He frowned, waiting for me to say more. "He doesn't seem the type to scroll his weekend away. He tinkers, just like many of our fathers did. One minute he's in the garage looking for a tool, then he's putting up a shelf or topping up the cars with oil and screen wash. Always tinkering. I bet he doesn't even have social media – and if he does, his version is more like a newspaper," I said, scoffing my black cherry jam on toast and finishing my coffee before we headed out.

That same weekend, while cleaning the back of the wardrobe, I pushed my finger straight through the skirting board. We had a leak, and it must have been happening for a while. The symbolism didn't pass me by, but the practical side of me decided to wait until my husband got home. Tempting as it was to take a sledgehammer to the wall dividing the wardrobe and the ensuite, I resisted.

A couple of hours later he walked through the door, golf clubs in hand. I mentioned that at some point we'd need to look into why the bottom of the wall was damp. Less than ten minutes after walking through the door, half the dividing wall was down. Broken tiles lay scattered across the ensuite floor. As we cleared the space — Ashley still in his golfing gear, me clutching a cup of coffee, I realised the familiar pattern of men and women was playing out.

I wanted to know what the previous owners had done to cover this up: to trace the story back, to notice the cleverly placed sealant and patchwork. Ashley, meanwhile, was already planning the repairs — who we could call, what steps we'd need to take. Sometimes we don't need something fixed at all, we just need someone to listen, to hold the story of the problem before rushing to repair it.

In the first years of our marriage, I created space for my husband to tell me stories and encouraged him to expand on them. I asked about his day, but also how it felt, how his colleague was coping, how his family member was doing. It didn't come naturally to him at first.

I often think back to the first night we reconnected after school. He told me stories of Iraq and of brotherhood, of loss and of love. He pulled up photos on his laptop, even regimental tour videos. I knew these stories came from deep within his heart because I felt them. Stories told in truth always land differently. That night, I knew I was witnessing one of those rare moments where deep stories are shared.

More than twenty years together now, I know he has taught me countless practical skills. When he is fixing something, he never tries to put me off watching or asking questions. One of my favourite things to do is to send him a photo of the tape measure, or any sort of tool from the garage with zero context, just to see how he reacts to what I might be up to; there is nothing like a little panic text in the middle of a work meeting to remind you that you are alive!

It should also be said that just because I can do things alone, it doesn't diminish him from his traditional masculine role, and perhaps that is our kind of fluidity within our relationship?

We can both be storytellers or skills sharers, even though there is one we predominantly prefer and thrive at. He worked as a chef for several years, so in many ways he taught me to cook. And I believe – often unknowingly – I taught him to walk more deeply through his stories, to share them more openly with friends in spaces beyond our home. This isn't just something in our household. It comes up again and again.

As women, we are encouraged from a young age to build connections: to make friends at the park and invite each other for tea. We are encouraged to connect through stories. But for boys, it's different. They play sports or video games. They take and leave it all on the pitch or the screen. They are rarely encouraged to share their more profound thoughts and feelings, because they are taught to share skills.

Whilst editing this chapter, my friend Yvonne and I talked about this concept and she laughed because she and her husband had new friends coming to visit, and her friend's husband had said he was "bringing his tool kit." *Classic skill sharing*, I thought. This silent separation of how we connect doesn't just build invisible walls in adult relationships with women; it isolates men from each other as well. Men need to share their stories, and women need to stop worrying that sharing their skills will mean they somehow lose.

Over the years, my husband has shared something with me, and I know he won't mind me sharing it with you. He told me that most men don't connect the way women do. They are raised to compete, just as young girls were once raised to provide. At that moment, I saw why it is important for men to root into their emotions and triggers the same way women have always done, because we need solid foundations for us all to be able to create new ways of living.

One summer after the lockdowns, we went to a home education camp not far from where we lived. Over 100 tents gathered, everyone hungry for community and connection after months of isolation. Each day began with a morning meeting where attendees offered up their skills, and a schedule unfolded: crafting, foraging, creating, small gatherings, or long walks through the woods.

There I saw the same pattern play out and shift on a larger scale. The women who shared both their skills and their stories seemed the most balanced. Their families seemed happiest. Their lines of communication stretched openly through generations, their stories and skills passing along like heirlooms. I watched a local farmer – now a dear friend – sit at her spinning wheel, stacks of yarn and wool at her feet, gently prompting my daughter to knit.

To the right, under a parachute canopy, two men carved spoons, teaching a small group of boys. There were only a handful of men at camp, yet those few were the ones most often sharing their skills during the day and their stories – loud, playful, heartfelt – around the fire at night. As if the fire itself was calling them back to a primal knowing: that men's stories are still needed in our communities, now more than ever.

For women, we crave stories. For men, I often see reluctance – they need coaxing to share the details. Yet around the fire, without screens or desks in the way, the old patterns return. For women, the gap often shows up in skills.

Too many of us have forgotten our most primal, life-giving ones – the ones our grandmothers knew. Instead we often share success stories or beauty tips. These have their place, but they are not the essential offerings the world is hungry for. Stories and skills must cross gender and age. They need to return in their most original, elemental form for the good of all. If men could reclaim their inner storytellers, and women could remember the potency of their oldest skills, what a world of potential that would be.

I've noticed this pattern everywhere. Men often dismiss women's talk as gossip, but gossip is not story. Stories hold a narrative power rooted in truth; gossip twists power into control. True power comes when we share our stories honestly with the people we love, trusting them to hold them, no control required.

Likewise, women complain that men rarely know what's going on in their male friends' lives until it's too late, or they only hear through their wives. And women, for our part, are rarely taught to share skills with each other anymore, not in the way those were once passed down by mothers and grandmothers. In short, there is a level of *not sharing* for all of us. Men fear being emasculated; women fear being shamed for not knowing how to change a fuse or refill washer fluid.

Imagine, just for a moment, a world where men tell their stories with the emotion and grace they've long been scorned for — and women share their skills not just with daughters or best friends, but with neighbours, with the village beyond. We can hold both, we can carry both, yet the world seems to have forgotten.

Heart Thread — I believe our relationships are built to share stories and skills. One is often labelled feminine, the other masculine. But we need both. All of us need both. Not only to rebuild our sense of community, but to reweave the deeper connection humanity and the planet are craving.

THE BODY REMEMBERS

I stood in the changing room and sobbed into my hands. I didn't have time for this! I had two children in the car and we had somewhere to be. I took my item number, clicked back to the assistant and walked to the check out, now a shell of myself from when I walked in.

I was moving up not one but two clothes sizes and it felt awful. This was the first time this happened. I remember getting into the car and Ashley immediately knowing something was wrong. One baby asleep in his carseat and the other toddler dozing by his side I confessed: "I don't recognise myself anymore. Who even am I?" He quickly reminded me not only had I had a baby two weeks ago, but also that bodies change and maybe it was time to throw out some of those clothes I've had since I was eighteen.

But I loved my body. I loved my little dimple twins at the base of my back, I loved the fact my mermaid thighs were a size bigger than my upper body, I loved the fact my scar on my little finger ached sometimes, like the scar of a sorcerer reminding me who the hell I was even at my most tired. I loved the way my hazel eyes twinkled when I laughed, and I was OK with having a bigger nose and big feet. What I wasn't OK with was that, at this point of being most vulnerable, after creating new life, I couldn't seem to root back into this new version of my body at any point; not who she was now –

leaking milk in the carpark of the shopping centre — and I had no clue who she was becoming and no choice but to surrender.

This was the first time I felt the peculiar disconnect from my body and led to a journey of rather a few years which I spent trying to regain some sort of understanding of this fleshy shell that holds my soul.

The voice of our body is one we don't really tend to acknowledge until something goes wrong. Sometimes something blocks the process or limits the function of this shell that transports us around and then, only then, do we listen. Even then, do we really listen to it? Or do we silence it with medication first? I'm not against modern medicine, however a brain like mine always wants to know the 'why' before we focus on distracting or muffling the communications of the body.

Our bodies are always showing up to call us in little ways. An example I remember that wasn't my own was the full body rash my son developed when he started school. I kept diaries, I changed wash powder, stripped bedding, tried creams and multiple doctors visits until his body confirmed what I had suspected during those months of lockdowns and no school. The rash was stress related; his body was showing me — and him — he was in an environment that did not feel safe.

The same way my husband's skin reacts when he eats too much sugar, or how my stomach tells me I'm walking near the edges of my nervous system. Our bodies have voices and they are ones we have silenced amongst the noise of today.

Only last week I was stood in my friend's kitchen as she washed a pot and I made the tea. I said out loud, "What do you need today?" as I flicked through her herbal tea supplies. That doesn't always need to be said for all to hear or shared with others, but it does need to be taken into account. I do this throughout my day and I trust my body to lead me towards what is good for us/her.

The first time I ever witnessed someone consider what they wanted, what their body wanted, and verbalise it was a few summers ago. Sat around the kitchen table over pastries and coffee, before making plans we did the usual when you live in the UK; we checked the weather. As the menfolk did this, I asked my friend what she wanted to do today. She contemplated the question and declared, "I don't mind, but I need trees," as if it was the most normal request in the world.

She listened to her body, knowing it makes sounds and her gut twists at different ideas. I learnt from that day that one of the essential ways to support my nervous system was to ask my body what it needed each day.

The same way our bodies tell us what is good for us, our bodies often remember things our mind have locked away. An example of this for me is that, on 13th April and 19th August I will often wake up and feel out of sorts, and if I don't go online I can spend a couple of hours waiting for the penny to drop. Then I realise it's the anniversary of my childhood friends' passing and my body remembers those losses. I haven't forgotten them – if you knew Todd King or Debbie Wade you would know forgetting them is impossible – but that feeling in my body resurfaces more often than not before my brain has realised the date.

So how do we listen to those voices? A dance to release something stuck inside you is one of my favourite ways – the body moving in place of speech. Or asking; asking your body what it needs, what's going on and listening. It's an intuitive pathway that can often work hand in hand with traditional and modern medicine.

Our bodies are always talking to us. From those moments when your hands shake; the tremor itself was your voice, speaking what words could not to the feeling in our body when someone isn't exactly telling the truth, to the lack of weight in their words. We must listen to our bodies as they protect not only our organs, but our soul, and the gateway to hearing our soul? Well that's our intuition of course.

THE KNOWING THAT REMAINED

The voice of my intuition was always strong: *Don't go this way, go that way. Don't sleep at so-and-so's house. This book is next, get tickets here, and watch this movie.* You know, those usual hunches and gut feelings? That has always been crystal clear for me. In fact, it has always been so clear I don't think I fully realised until my late twenties that not everyone has maintained a deep trust with their intuition or the voices of spirit in their ear.

I've been known to chase things, so much so that as a teen, I once chased a convicted convict through a prison kitchen with a microphone because I thought he should come and join me on stage as a line dancer. Needless to say, the guards found this hilarious, but the prisoner did not.

I was a child and, in my defence, at that age I still believed all inmates wore stripey jumpsuits of black and white or maybe orange. My drive when I wanted something was unstoppable. So when we happened to find a bungalow in the middle of the countryside on the road with no name, just round the corner from Ashley's work, I jumped on it like a cat on a field mouse.

I wanted it so badly that I kept scrolling back to the same thing, and then I screenshot it to see it even when I didn't have a signal. It was all I thought about. I would move the chickens, and the sunshine would gleam through the windows. I would also be able to hear the birds when I was lying in the bath. Yes, there was a bath!! I put it out there to the universe, and I needed a bath because the mobile home we were living in only had a shower.

As soon as Ashley entered the door at the end of his shift, we bundled into the car and drove along the quiet lane to take a quick look at the property. Even though I had left the agency a message to express my interest, I just wanted to see it in case it wasn't as good as the photos had shown.

As we swung into the driveway, I knew this was the place. The land was so luscious and alive, I wanted to live there. We watched the chickens in the garden and agreed it would be perfect to have the extra room and a bigger garden. The following morning, I emailed the agency to request the application form and to book a viewing, whilst explaining I had already left a message the day before, which no one had seemed to have picked up yet. Can you tell I was super keen?

No reply for another day and the next day was Friday, so I called again and they gave me the local farmer's number whose house it was, saying it was probably easier to call him directly. I called and spoke to his wife, only to be told he was out with the sheep and would call me on Sunday.

Sunday came and went, and we finally had the paperwork sent out and a viewing booked for a few days' time. I was beyond excited, envisioning what I could do with the garden, perhaps a little veg plot or a deck so we could look out over the valley as the sun set across the fields.

We met the farmer, who explained we couldn't get into the property today as the tenant's dog would find it traumatic. We were disappointed but said we would look through the windows at the other end of the bungalow to get a general idea of the space.

As we knew, homes in this area did not come up often, so we signed the tenancy application and sent off our paperwork the following day, having been told there was a lot of interest, now all we could do was wait and trust that the universe would sort it for us.

A week passed, and I hadn't heard a thing. On Saturday, we decided we would just drive to the estate agent and say we were passing and wondered if there was an update. It turned out they had 'lost' our application. We had to go back through the paperwork again.

The following week, we managed to get a second viewing to hopefully see inside, as we pulled up to the lane the house was on, a woman from the village wound down her window and yelled, "Alright Ash! You don't want to live here, mate, the water runs down the walls and it's freezing!" We thanked her for the heads up and continued to the house. I didn't care. If I am honest, I thought she was out of her mind and had probably had a falling out with the old farmer or something that made her not want to move out.

I persisted. In the month since this property went on the market, we were none the wiser. Another four working days, and they requested further paperwork and asked if we could move in the next two weeks. I explained that, like most, we would have to give a month's notice on our current home, and if I had known sooner, then it would have been possible. A later date was agreed, and that was that. I got what I wanted. Ignoring all of the stop signs, red flags and unnecessarily complicated hurdles, I persisted.

Moving day arrived and as Ashley's Dad pulled onto the drive with the trailer, his face shifted as he said: "This place has no damp proofing, hope it's got some log files in there, Char." It did not. I quickly realised I had been pushing against the universe for something that was not meant for us.

The walls did in fact, run with water and then freeze in the winter. We lost large amounts of furniture and belongings during the time we were stuck there. However, we put a smile on our faces and persisted. Lesson learnt. Trust that all things happen as they are supposed to.

This wasn't the first or the last time I had been too headstrong for my own good and pushed for something that was never meant to be for me or my highest good. I went for jobs, houses, and holidays that were total disasters, then more minor things that we won't get into. But no matter how big or small, I ignored my intuition over something I thought I wanted without trusting the universe to bring me something even better.

The red flags I ignored, the signposts I drove past, the blocks in my pathway. I steamrolled through them, thinking I knew best and, guess what? I didn't. I knew I deserved better, but I didn't trust enough to let it unfold for me. I pushed, and pushing is never the best idea, because you can't force something that was never meant to work for you.

As I watched the water freeze outside and we wore clothes to bed to keep warm that winter, I swore I would never push the universe to bend to my will again. It knew best, it saw further than I could. I promised spirit I would trust them as far as my human mind could, and we never looked back.

My intuition has always been strong when I listen to it. Possibly because I didn't ever fully share where my wisdom was coming from until my later twenties. In some ways I kept my internal compass intact; a secret between me, myself and I. From those classroom history lessons to friendships and work projects. It began with simple statements: "My gut just knows", or "My gut says yes". This was way before I looked into the science of it or knew what energy was. My body has been leading me for longer than I realised. The voice of intuition is often one that speaks in repetitive patterns.

Synchronicity has been one of those patterns that I have always been able to pick up on. Some might say it comes from silently counting how many pints your step-dad was on, an awareness born out of protection. Others might call it a diversity of sorts, for me, it doesn't matter.

I have so many times been guided by moments where strange things had unfolded in ways too precise to be a coincidence. We could have possibly written an entire book on these moments alone. Like the New Year's Eve when a rogue firework sparked against my skin, and I screamed, "I'm on fire!!" as the wind blew in between the homemade garden canopies and a pool of rainwater sloshed over me from head to toe, putting out the flames in an instant.

Even before that, there was Myra Wooten, the woman who showed up in our family's lives when we needed her most. With her purple Fiesta and warm heart, she brought light into our home during some of its most difficult times of emotional inconsistency and rebuilding. She reminded me how much joy was possible, even when everything else felt heavy and complex. This realisation didn't come to me until my thirties; how she slotted into the family just well enough to support us without imposing. She was a gift I will always be grateful for.

We also had a cat appear when we were children. It wasn't claimed, so we adopted it and it lived with us for many years. I do wonder now if it happened to appear when we also needed some extra comfort after my father had left.

You will not notice everything the universe whispers; sometimes, it's so tiny it takes years or a revisit of a journal. Other times, it's massive, and everyone sees it. Looking back on the years, somehow we have always gotten by and managed to complete the things we set out to do without too much trouble. Even just this morning, I thought that the gold on my kettle was peeling for some reason and that it might be leaking water. Less than two hours later, my friend texted asking if I wanted a kettle as she had two new ones and needed only one. Thank you, universe, I'll take it!

My intuition has always been there, sending me people, lessons, and moments of knowing. It might appear that I have always been the person who just *knew* things. I can't take credit for half the advice I gave as a kid. I knew who was lying. I knew when people weren't telling the whole story. My energy radar never failed me.

Heart Thread — Like so many things, the voice of intuition is a muscle. It takes practice and buckets of trust. Yet it doesn't take a massive leap or declaration. Simply acknowledging this knowing within yourself is often the key that turns the lock and opens the door. And then you begin to ask the questions. How the answers show up? Well, that's all part of the fun.

And it is often our intuition that first knows the difference between words that carry truth, and words that are empty.

THE COURAGE TO SPEAK WITHOUT WISDOM

During the writing process I met a man called Howard. Not like that, calm yourself. Howard is our local garage door repairman. Talking to him briefly on the driveway one morning, I saw he had a big heart and an integrity I admired. We talked about children, the local community, garage doors and all the things in between whilst I made him a coffee. He told me about his wife, and then we hit that point where he asked me what I do. I said I was halfway through writing a book about my life. He smiled and said, "That's the thing about life. At twenty-five you think you have it all figured out, at thirty-five you think you know it all, only to realise at fifty that you still have some things to learn."

I smiled and nodded, paid the man and he was on his way. But that conversation stayed with me for a few days because, on some level Howard was not wrong. We do quite often think we have seen and heard it all only to turn around eight years later and be knocked back down with a huge realisation that things aren't always as you had originally thought or that we aren't the very same person we were before.

When did we forget that wisdom is in our bones, I wondered. Is there really a time in our existence where we step into wisdom fully? A parade or presentation where we receive an official badge of 'wisdom' that declares to others: "I have something worth listening to!" Or is the voice of wisdom something we always carry, it's just the world distracts us and we forget that lessons in life aren't failures, there is wisdom there too.

It made me have a few days of wobbling and avoiding the laptop if I am honest. I was approaching forty and somehow now was wondering if I had enough wisdom, knowledge or awareness to write a book that might be helpful. Then I remembered: You can be two things at once. You can be the fire and the water, you can root into the ground so deeply that you are unbreakable and yet you can choose to continue to sway with the wind. Wasn't that what this book was about?

For nearly forty years, I have carried so many things that were not mine, stood on mountain tops watching a world lose its connection to each other and its land. I have rallied for people to speak up, and protected so many who do not feel ready to defend themselves, until I ended up metaphorically bloody and exhausted and somehow no matter how many people say to me, "You are so wise Char," I don't seem to fully believe it. Why?

Firstly because I needed to learn these things – a lot of them the hard way. And secondly because I always believed in something bigger than myself; something to learn, or better understand, something to grow from. That's why.

When wisdom speaks, it doesn't ask to be heard. It becomes the ground you stand on.

Wisdom is not the voice that comes last. It is simply the voice that is willing to listen before it speaks. Sometimes that's to a friend, colleague, their own intuition or the land beneath their feet.

We so often think of wisdom as an elder; grey-haired, bone-worn, slow to rise and last to speak in the room as the penny drops around the table. But

I have met wisdom in children, in the wind and in those cracks of broken breath between those final heartbeats of the people I love.

Wisdom is not the same as intellect. It's not always loud like outrage, or polished into a confident presentation. Wisdom isn't a witty one-liner or clever commentary. It's deep rooted and slow burning throughout every lifetime from beginning to end and back around again.

Wisdom can come through the teenager who names what no one else will; through the woman who left the room when her body said no; through the mother who says, "I don't know, but I'll find out". Wisdom will continue to show up in the places we least expect it. How do I know this? Because the voice of wisdom speaks from memory. Sometimes it's personal, often its ancestral and once spoken it's eternal – floating out into the ether.

Wisdom is the voice that holds both grief and grace in the same sentence. Wisdom is the voice that doesn't rush to answer, because it trusts the question to teach. Wisdom is often the voice that breaks silence not to shatter it, but to mend it.

We don't only grow into wisdom by ageing, we grow into it by listening, and embody wisdom by being still enough to hear what lives beneath our reactions. By speaking *after* the truth has passed through your bones. And when you find that voice – your wise voice – you'll know it by its weight. Not heavy like a burden, but holy like sacred metal.

You will speak and not need applause.
You will be misunderstood and still feel at peace.
You will say less – and mean more.

Wisdom is the truth that no longer needs defense. Wisdom does not demand to be heard or wait to be recognised. It simply is.

Stevie Nicks once said: "Your graciousness is what carries you. It isn't how old you are, how young you are or how beautiful, it's what comes out of your heart. If you have graciousness you have won the game." And perhaps that goes for being gracious when it comes to the idea of wisdom as well.

So let's move forward with grace and turn the page to part two.

A rebel's cry for devotion

I have run with the wild,
fought with fire,
worn defiance like armour,
And let the world know my name in thunder.

But even the fiercest storm longs for quiet.
Even the untamed heart craves something worth staying for.

So hear me now –
Not in surrender, but in choice.
Not in chains, but in love.

I do not kneel because I am broken.
I kneel because I have found something greater than myself.
Something worth my hands unclenched,
my walls undone,
My ashes repurposed – not for war, but for collaboration.

Let my devotion be as bold as my rebellion.
Let me burn not just to defy but to illuminate.

Even when crowned I am still wild, I am still free.
But this fire – this flame I will not walk away from, I will carry it forward within for she burns for something more than war.

Let that flame of knowing be enough,

THE TIME FOR HOLLOW WORDS IS OVER

I've heard every type of voice going in almost every type of setting. I've sat in silence watching people shrink at another's words under the guise of the room not being a safe space and the guise of nothing needs to be fixed because no one is broken. I've heard people say the wisest person in the room speaks last and the most confident person in the room is often the weakest.

I've heard people say that extroverts need to give introverted people a chance to speak, it does the rounds online every once in a while and makes me shudder. Because I've invited people to share in spaces when they are quiet, I've buffered and mopped up misunderstandings over and over again and then come home and had to give my body days to recover and reset from the cortisol spike, I have been intimidated and I have been told I have been person who has been doing the intimidating.

I've felt shame for my words and shame for my silence. And I have lost count of the times my words have changed others' lives. I don't say that out of ego, I say it because I have read my yearbook, I've received the cards in the post and the Facebook or WhatsApp messages thanking me for words I forgot I had said, and yet those words I quickly cast out on breathe, those words have saved a life or broken a cycle of trauma that I wasn't always aware of at the time. These restraints are all bullshit. Because every single environment and voice is different.

I've sat in meetings, watched in restaurants and concerts the power of a single voice, and it never ceases to amaze me how one voice can change the world energetically and emotionally. I am devoted to making humanity a better place by the time I fly off to another life in the small ways and the big and I know that we all want to be seen, loved, heard and remembered. And my god that's all I have ever dreamed of for those people who are close to my heart and for that reason alone, we need to talk about hollow words.

And that means we cannot pretend that all voices deserve to be heard, not at the moment at least. Does everyone have a right to speak? Of course. But what we need is discernment. Discernment that sometimes the person in front of you is just telling you what you want to hear. That sometimes a person promises to protect you their entire life, and it turns out they can't make it past the first twenty years; or a partner who says they love you knowing they are secretly calling another woman late at night.

Not all promises we speak are untrue. Not all, but some, in fact many can be. And that's for a number of reasons. Sometimes it's that we play into this collective vision of how we think each of us should be. Other times we want to believe that words that we speak hold weight — we really wish it so, but we haven't done the work on the inside to keep those words from being full of nothing more than thin air that slowly leaks until you are left quite surprised that that person's words have fallen flat.

That's a hard one to spot, because when you stand opposite someone you love and wish the words they were saying were true, you wish they would be able to keep their word, but in your core you know they can't. Those are the hardest ones.

There are, however, those who speak hollow words — you know the ones. They are the voices that are far too concerned with their appearance to the outside world than the words they use in their own homes. They are the ones who more often than not will play the victim when the truth of their actions are almost becoming too close to the surface of reality or public perception. Because public perception is the priority.

There's the corporate speak with no follow-through, apologies with no behavior change, words used to manipulate empathy — all hollow. Who holds the hollow voice accountable? What is our responsibility as listeners on the receiving end of these words that are, quite frankly, thrown at us from every angle in what often feels like a waste land of a world of social media's hollow messaging, influencer culture and political doublespeak?

I could sense when someone was spinning a tale for something beyond entertainment. I used to say "I don't like them". Truth was at the time I didn't have the words for it. Now I do.

Those times when I used to think I was a bitch? Turns out I had an intuition and an inner knowing. I could sniff out a lie wrapped in charm, a smile hiding an agenda or a compliment meant to disarm; I just didn't have the language back then to explain it fully. So I let others call it being difficult, too much or too sensitive. But now I know — it was clarity and energy before evidence.

Hollow voices are the voices that say things out of personal intention, sometimes out of protection or to create a false sense of self, and not everyone knows they are doing it.
The worst ones are the voices that root into another's weakness or focus on their perception and effect.

How will you know when you hear those words, you ask? It took me a while to figure this out. And the truth is you just know, your gut tells you there is more to what is coming out of their mouth. Words, you feel. Even if they hurt or they are direct. You feel them, you feel their intention and their purpose.

The question I have wondered is can hollow speakers transform – and how? I really hope that with accountability and a shift in choosing where we listen it can, yes, because this is so much bigger than our quick action to label everyone as narcissistic. Can the hollow voices in the world change?

One: Do they want to? Because it starts with integrity; everyone needs to bridge the gap between alignment of word and action.

Two: Are they prepared to make the choice and go against fear? In a world where we are told we have such a beauty of choice, choice is one of the scariest things; and choosing to speak is possibly one of the scariest. And yet the thing that limits voice, well the thing that limits the world in its entirety, is fear and all the disguises it shows up in. Fear is the only thing in the way.

It is only now I know my voice has never been hollow, it has been ungrounded. But now it is firmly rooted. It's taken me to swing from both sides of the scale and back to the middle to understand this. (heads up: It will continue to swing because I am human). And, as a human being I'll continue to have to sit and watch people I love struggle to find their own voice, muddle through their own emotions and words.

I have no doubt there will always be someone speaking badly of me as well. Let them carry on, because the only words that matter are the words that carry weight. Not the weight where we then carry others' words on our shoulders, no no. The words we feel inside when someone says them; the words the speaker embodies and lives rather than the empty quotes they post online for sympathy.

My husband used to say to me, "You don't say anything you don't mean" and somehow, sitting here now, that lands more deeply. Because he is right, I'd rather sit in silence than tell a lie; I'd rather leave the room than listen to another man talk down to a woman so that he feels good about himself, and I won't do it dramatically or quietly: "This conversation is making me feel uncomfortable I am leaving".

It's simple: We do not have to fix everything for everyone because people need to learn to speak for themselves eventually, but also we do not need to ignore the conversations in front of us.

My words might be loud and sometimes a little messy or emotional, but they will never be hollow. Never.

Our words need to be embodied. We need to have awkward conversations, say things, call a friend. Not from a place of anger or trying to prove people wrong, but from a place of wanting us all to live in a better world. It sounds cheesy, doesn't it? But it's true, and I feel it in every bone of my body. We need to listen more deeply and stop sharing hollow words. If we don't mean it, don't say it.

There is never going to be a perfect way of doing this. There are, however, a million different ways to keep the gateways of communication open.

There is a balance and an awareness that is needed in this world. How do we do that? I'm not sure; every conversation is so individual that I would be foolish to try and wash them with a single solution.

However the words that matter, the words that take us into better worlds – worlds I hope my children get to see, are the worlds where our words hold weight and our voices are carried with devotional hearts.

What kind of voice do you want to be?

The time of the hollow word is up.

Your words have been weighed
Your words have been measured,
and they absolutely have been found wanting.
Welcome to the New World, where wisdom speaks,
not to simply be heard, but to become the ground that the future is built from.

THE PRESENCE OF SPIRIT

This chapter is a meeting point of two worlds in my life. Literally a crossing of a veil that I walk daily with one foot in one world and one in the other. Life is very much an accumulation of choices and here is a small one for you: 1. You can choose to read on with an open heart and an open mind; or 2. You skip this part and hop straight over to the voice of ancestry. I'm not here to convince anyone of anything, and yet the truth is we can all talk to spirit and/or source if we choose to.

With that in mind I very much hope you will go with option one.

When I began writing this book, I carried more than 20,000 words on my life with Spirit. In the end, I filed them away, perhaps for another project, another time. Yet something in my core whispered that without at least a nod to Spirit, this book would be missing not just a part of my life, but a glimpse of what is possible for humanity.

There is, of course, a heavy misconception around this. For many, it is a punchline, the butt of a joke: people who believe they can talk to the dead, or to realms beyond sight. But the truth is that this way of listening requires deep rootedness, a groundedness as steady as stone. It is less about leaving this world than it is about being fully present in it — while knowing there is more.

I know some will roll their eyes at this. Spirit-talk is often met with a smirk, a joke, or a polite silence. But to cut Spirit out of my story would be to cut away half of my life.

So I name it anyway. Not to convince you. Not to prove anything. But because naming it is an act of courage. It is a way of saying: this too is a real voice and one we can not only all tune into but learn from and carry forward. The first time I can remember seeing spirit? Well that's an easy one.

My tiny, five-year-old little fingers clutched the duvet with sweaty palms, and my eyes squeezed shut. I knew the man on the landing was back.

I always knew he was male, though I didn't understand why he was there or why he never spoke. Couldn't everyone see him?! The moment I asked, I wasn't sure if I felt or heard the word *no*. It floated across the air and landed inside me, and I *knew* it was true.

I heard my parents coming up the stairs. It must be late, I thought. Why didn't they rush for the pull cord in the bathroom like I did? I stifled a giggle at the idea of my Dad being afraid of the dark or the man at the top of the stairs. My Dad was afraid of nothing. The man must be OK if he could walk past the man on the stairs without a second thought.

I took a deep breath, puffing out my chest and trying to be brave. But I wasn't sure which scared me most; the spirit I could see or the possibility of more lurking in the dark. In my five-year-old mind, the solution was simple: roll over, tuck the duvet up under my chin, and hope it all went away.

It didn't. The voice indeed never left, I just became more distracted. Like so many of us, the voices became muffled and the visions blurred by the noise of everyday life.

For as long as I can remember, there has been more than one voice in my head, The first one is mine — the highest version of me. She is calm and wise; she speaks in a steady rhythm like a drum, not in any rush for anything. The second is my human self; the voice that can easily be focused on the worst-case scenario and the trivial or dramatic of day-to-day life. And then there is another, mostly a quieter one, the third voice I have come to know as the voice of spirit.

Some days one is louder than the other, but much like music, one way or another the voice of spirit has been with me always.

However, I was about eight years old the first time I can remember hearing an actual voice other than aspects of myself. This voice was not loud like the voices of authority that demanded obedience, and I expect it was easier to hear when I was so young, before the whispers of doubt from the outside would enter. The same way a lot of us have invisible friends when we are young, before anyone could stamp it out with three simple words: That's not normal.

One day in the summer holidays I was walking ahead of my family around Chew Valley Lake, watching the sunlight play on the surface of the water and not at all paying attention to my feet. Singing Ace of Base, *Don't Turn Around* quietly to myself with not a care in the world, I had somehow walked quickly out of sight.

As I approached a tree, I heard my name being called in an unfamiliar voice. Fear froze my feet to the ground. Looking over my shoulder and listening again, I heard nothing. Clearly, it wasn't my mother or one of the boys calling me.

As I turned to face the direction I was heading, our eyes met and I screamed so loudly that my mother thought I was being attacked! The female adder simply moved from the base of the tree in the middle of the footpath back towards the woodlands in her slow and steady locomotion. By the time they came running around the bend, she was gone. I didn't need to pull my country walks book from my rucksack to know what she was; her brown zig zags and red eyes told me all I needed to know.

Once I had calmed down we continued to walk and, from then on, I stayed near an adult. I'm not sure if anyone believed I had seen it. In fact, over the years, I don't think I have even asked about it. I do wonder now if I was screaming because it was an adder, or if I was screaming because she was calling my name. I never told a soul about this until now.

Many years on, I now know the man on the stairs was my Gramps. When I was very young, he never came too close or spoke too much. He'd send me songs or nudge me toward the dartboard. Sometimes, he'd simply smile when I was scared; a quiet presence, steady as ever.

As a child, my connection with spirit strengthened to the point that I would run through the lane between our house in Ashwicke and up the stairs whilst stretching my hand out for the bathroom light; it felt like someone had removed all the air in those types of spaces or that invisible walls boxed me in. Until I understood what was happening, I would simply hold my breath and run.

As the outside world of voices crowded in and without even realising it, I stopped listening as much; stopped seeing as clearly. The voice of knowing spirit never left, but I let the world drown it out and replaced it, like so many of us do — with tools.

As an adult I have learnt to listen again. These voices are not loud. They are not theatrical. They are steady, ancient, and persistent. And they have walked beside me long enough that to deny them now would feel like denying my own heartbeat.

And so I speak of Spirit not to convince, but to witness.

Because naming it aloud is part of my own voice — my own story — and to deny it would be to silence a piece of myself I refuse to lose.

Spirit walks with me in daily life, in small moments as much as the profound. It is in the windchime that sounds when there is no breeze, the rhythm of change in the waves on the shore, the smell of familiar family members across the kitchen table, the memory of ancestors pressing through my veins and the pause in the quiet pause between breaths.

This voice of Spirit is not separate from me. It is a thread woven into every choice I make, not leading, but guiding, because there is a difference. Every word I speak, every step I take they are there. And like all voices worth listening to, it asks only one thing: that I show up fully, that I pay attention, and that I have the courage to name it, even when many choose not to believe.

Heart thread – Notice your own threads of voice – however subtle, however fleeting. They may appear in the hum of a song, a memory, a whisper, or a pulse beneath your feet. And if you dare to name them, you may find that the world is speaking to you in ways you never expected.

THE ECHOES THAT MADE ME

The voice of ancestry is for everyone, family circumstances are irrelevant.

The voice of ancestry is one I have mixed views on. I always felt something was missing, but I could never quite put my finger on what. The only conclusion I can share is that I don't believe one particular person or situation caused this feeling. I think it was an extensive list of things, and blaming a marriage, household, or external circumstance doesn't change the result, which was that, like so many others, I didn't always feel understood or fully seen in my family.

Over the years, I continued writing myself the letters of wisdom I longed for. Comforting words to keep trying or firm fairness to let something go. The wisdom that is usually spoken out loud or shared down the family line; yet, for me, out of shame I couldn't ask for what I needed. I would use encouraging words that I needed to hear through all phases and celebrations of life.

At one point, I wondered if I would share them, and somehow, they simply felt as if they were for my eyes only. Letters on the days I found out I was pregnant, a letter when we went into lockdown, a letter when my daughter turned thirteen; on the days that felt hard and, of course, on those days when something amazing happened and I felt as if I didn't have anyone to call or share my news with. Some might say I wrote what I needed to hear; others might believe I wrote them from a circle of ancestors who knew me well and loved me dearly beyond the grave.

It wasn't that I didn't have a family. I did, inside and outside my home. I had my Dad, whom I love dearly, and yet we often see the world very differently at the best of times. I have siblings, but I am still the oldest, and calling randomly to share is not something we have ever done. You can have family and not fully know them, so letter writing to myself and for myself was the way for me.

One night, I wrote a letter to my dying grandmother. It happened as most others did; I had no intention beforehand that this would be the day. I had been burning a candle for her for over a week now, feeling she was in the corridor between worlds. I didn't know what else I could do until I went to bed early one night and found myself writing her a letter.

I wrote about the times we were at the allotment when I was a child; I reminded her of her friends we used to visit and laughed about when she would stop and talk to me and my friends through the railings at school during summer lunchtimes, even when the dinner lady told us to come away.

I wrote all the things I wished she had known before it was too late. As the emotions washed over me, I reminded her she could go when she was ready, she could leave, and she could be with my grandad again. Not out of permission, but more confirmation I suppose. I blew out the candle, pulled the duvet up high, and drifted off into a deep sleep.

The night my grandmother passed away, I was so broken that I could not speak at the other end of the phone. It felt as if the missing link to those heart-led women I had always felt had been passed over to me as I gripped the phone, unable to find any words. My chest began to expand until I heard it crack, and the world almost seemed to tilt on its axis. Suddenly, I saw myself standing on the edge of a cliff top, holding a lantern of guardianship I had never perceived I would be holding. Little did I realise, as I was taking this new role, that the others in my family were gathering in their metaphorical boats, ready to leave.

I lost four generations of women in one night. My punishment for silence was disownment.

I had been burned so many times for my use of words, but never had I expected to be sent up in flames for my grief-stricken lack of them. I felt like a porcelain doll that had been smashed onto the rocks at the edge of that cliff I had been standing upon, as I was blocked, deleted and told not to attend the funeral.

Beyond the pain of this severing there was a deeper thought process that I needed to look at under my mental microscope. I was being punished for the first time in my life (that I could recall) for my silence. Because in the moment my heart broke on one end of the phone I didn't immediately ask about anyone else. This made me "selfish and an embarrassment to my family"; the words amongst others that whispered in my ear every night for some time when I tried to sleep.

Me. Selfish. The first person in most rooms to notice anyone struggling, the first person to offer to take a photo of a couple on a day trip, the first one to give up her seat, text a friend or offer to help. I was selfish for not using my voice to check in on someone else.

As I sat on the floor scribbling down everything that had been said on the phone, my husband begged me to get some rest. It was 2 a.m., and I could feel pieces of myself sinking to the bottom of the ocean floor. Still, some small part of me knew that one day, I'd have to call each of those pieces back. I needed these words — the ones thrown at me through grief and pain out of my body and onto the page.

Lucky for me, I'm a researcher. And much to my husband's dismay, I stayed up until 4 a.m., recording it all. He sat beside me and didn't ask more than once, "Why?" My answer, even through the sharpest of pain: "Because there's a lesson I'm supposed to learn here. Tomorrow I'll be too numb to realise it, but one day, I'll need these words, to remind me, to fuel me, to help me figure it all out." I knew I'd spin them into gold one day. Not now. Not soon. But someday. Even then, that tiny flame inside me knew.

The next day, I got out of bed and decided I would wrap myself up into a ball for a while. It wasn't the world that had broken me, it was my family; something you don't ever expect to happen, no matter how many myths and stories of legend you have read. I no longer thought I was a good person; I no longer thought I was capable of making the right decision.

I had been banished, not allowed to attend the funeral and cut off from contact. I was stuck in a spiral of every mistake I had ever made, over and over again on repeat, until that very night. I was engulfed in a macro version of grief, and when that happens, you should have a plan and a guide. I didn't feel like I had either.

For the first time in my life I didn't follow up. I didn't try to fix anything about how anyone perceived me. Which is the entire opposite of the way I was raised. I figured if I could survive distant relatives' comments online about me and I could allow my family to speak about me in whatever way they chose, then I was eventually going to become bullet proof for the future. So I let them talk.

The one thing I did notice, something that to this day still feels like a very old and yet deep bruise, is that no one asked for my side of things. Not a message, an email or telephone call to say, " Hey Charlie, what happened here? Because it feels off." So often we believe the first version of a story we hear in the world; I guess that is what they call "getting ahead of the press". I chose to let them roll out the papers and write what they wanted, and they still do. Sometimes you have to live the life of a villain. The power comes when you understand the villain isn't always as bad as you were told in the fairytale.

Thirty plus years of putting the outside world before myself, yet I was now standing alone and abandoned, all because my pain took precedence for a minute or two. My pain took my voice in its clutches, and all that was left was silence.

Like Little Red Riding Hood I felt like I was in the woods running from the beast, only there was no lineage of washerwomen on this side of the veil to pull me across the water into my power. Curling up in a ball felt like the safest and best option at the time, I just needed to promise myself that this spot on the forest floor was a temporary resting place. There were those wild parts of me who wanted to claw back the 'screw the world' teenage part of myself, yet there was also concern that the last time I went through that I destroyed a lot of things I loved. A small part of me carried the belief that they were right — I would die alone.

The presence of my children was the only thing that kept me here for a while. The mundane everyday routines kept me in my body as much as it possibly could, however I was functioning in automatic. I might have been shattered into pieces that night, with wounds that are some of my most profound. But the scars are a gift I now feel honoured to carry. Because picking up those pieces from the bottom of that ocean bead, I got to choose how I wanted to repattern myself for the future.

My grandmother was Doris Haycox. She was a force to be reckoned with. She had a tongue that could scar as much as it could soothe; she took no prisoners, and yet she gave her all to those she loved. I have never known someone so true to her beliefs, even if the facts were in front of her. If she had already picked a team, she followed them through to the end.

She had a spark about her that I couldn't possibly include in this book because I know I carry that same spark within me. You either love us or hate us. There is no glossy public version of us to perform in ways that people want to see. We call a spade a spade, and we are never backwards in coming forward. In that darkest time, this was the single spark of my ancestry that I could continue to carry forward on those hardest days.

It has been said by a few that I should never turn my back on my family but, you see, I didn't. That I should do the utmost to rebuild the connection that was severed that night. These people mean well, they really do, because it's uncomfortable to witness and I get it. Yet I know that even if given the opportunity, I couldn't go back. Because I know those new parts of me I have found simply wouldn't fit into the family puzzle I once lived in.

This was a type of grief I'm not sure I will ever be able to fully explain. Losing a grandparent through death and, the same night, further generations by choice was shattering, but to experience that level of pain stacked on top of each other was a new kind of grief I'm not sure I had heard anyone ever talk about.

I am eternally grateful that not one single person told me "people do strange things when they are hurting" or "family should stick together". Because all words and actions are eventually forgivable, and yet you cannot go back on them; what has been done is set in stone. Choosing not to forgive is voluntarily tying yourself to those boulders and you drown at the bottom of the ocean.

I can forgive, but there are some things I will never forget.

To begin with, I didn't want to talk about any of it. It was as if the lost words of that night were floating through me in grief and rage, yet I couldn't fully grasp any of them with the grace I needed to push them out of my mouth. I sent one identical text to my nearest and dearest, and that was that. I felt that there wasn't much else to say.

As blindsided as I had been, there was also a part of me, somewhere deep inside, that immediately felt acceptance, as if the impact wound was a spot of realisation that this was always going to happen. However, the bruised tissue around the outside was an entirely different story. She remembered that same feeling that little girl felt that eventually, everybody would leave.

It would be so easy for me to sit in victim mode. But somehow that feels like self betrayal and I refused to be in that loop of personal hell.

I was equal parts hurting and healing, which felt as if I was engulfed in a blue flame somewhere in between pain and rage, peace and acceptance. I knew I needed to be held with just the right amount of pressure, and yet every time I tried to open my mouth and speak, the same silence I was being punished and freed for was still there in the echoes. It wasn't that there were no offers. I am forever grateful to my friends who were there with their support at that time. It just felt as if a curse had been placed on my voice, I couldn't find the words I needed to share with even those closest to me.

Heart Thread – Your voice, your decision. Always. And not everyone is going to like that. Especially those who have seen you repeatedly pick them and others up, support entire communities and rarely need support yourself. When you take even the slightest step back for self preservation, there will be a response and that won't always be one of encouragement and support, but you need to do it anyway.

THE HOWL OF GRIEF

The howl of grief is such an individual one, almost impossible to capture, and yet it's something each of us will come to know. It's so tender that I wasn't sure I would include it here at all. For a long time, I questioned whether I had experienced enough grief to have the right to write about it. My dearest friend has recently lost her father and the pain in watching this, even only feeling it from a far is heartbreaking to witness. I'm not sure I have the words for those feelings either, but I will try.

I quite often look out across my life and the lives of those I love, I see grief is everywhere – in grand losses and in the smallest, most hidden corners.

People often say grief comes in waves. Others say it doesn't shrink over time. I have known the kind of grief that crashes in, leaving you unable to breathe, and I have known the quieter kind that simply lingers over the years, wishing for praise or love that will never come. Grief has a way of moving through the world and reshaping it over and over, and just when you think you know how to tend to grief, it shows up in your life in a new cosmic format.

We grieve the big things, of course; the deaths, the heartbreaks, the chapters that close so abruptly we are left standing in the doorway of what was. But I think we also grieve the small, often invisible losses; the disappointments and the friendships that fade without explanation, the jobs that once seemed like golden opportunities only to become cages.

And perhaps most deeply of all, we grieve the lives we never lived; who we thought we might become, the versions of ourselves we never grew into, the ways we feel we've let others down. These griefs are rarely spoken, but they live inside us nonetheless.

Every grief feels different to me. Losing someone I loved at a young age is not the same as letting go of a dream, and neither is the same as realizing a season of life has ended. Each has its own sharpness, its own quiet lessons. Todd King, for instance; his wit, his laugh, the way he could light up a whole room. Losing him left a hole that years have not filled.

Then of course there is Debbie Wade's absence, with her childlike joy and smiles, this is something I still carry. They were taken far too soon, and there are no words for the ache of losing people when you're still so very young. Those griefs never vanish; they simply become companions, shadows that walk beside me.

There are griefs that don't announce themselves so loudly. They slip into the middle of an ordinary day, leaving me inexplicably tender or restless. It's as if my body remembers before my mind does. The anniversary of a loss or a birthday, a date that still carries weight even when I haven't marked it on the calendar. We've talked about this before – how our body holds memory – but our soul carries it too, in ways my mind sometimes refuses to. Our souls remember and feel just deeply.

What makes grief even harder is how little space we give it in our culture. We speak of "moving on", as if grief is a task to be completed, a box to be checked. We disguise our grief as complaining. People ask how you're doing, but they rarely want the real answer, and so much grief gets swallowed into silence. I have learned to respect that silence, to let it be sacred. Not every grief needs words; some are meant to be held quietly, like fragile glass.

And yet, within grief, I have always found a paradox I didn't expect. Because grief, for all its sharpness, has a way of pointing me back toward joy. It feels strange, almost irreverent, to place those words together — grief and joy — but I can't untangle them. Grief is love with no place to go. And love, even when wounded, still has the power to turn us toward life.

When grief cracks me open, everything comes rushing in: rage, regret, tenderness, relief, fear, even laughter that bubbles up in the middle of tears. And strangely, that chaos is what reminds me I am alive. Grief strips away everything nonessential, leaving me face-to-face with what matters most: A bird's song, the hand of someone I love, the soft light of evening; things I once passed over without notice suddenly shine with a kind of holiness.

There is no one path through grief. Some losses soften after months, some after years, and some never fully leave us at all. But I no longer see grief as the end of a story. It is a teacher; sometimes the harshest we will ever know, but also the one that brings us back to the miracle of being alive. So I try to meet my grief with respect, even when it feels unbearable. I try to trust that it is shaping me in ways I cannot yet understand. And I try to remember that grief's voice, though painful, always carries love at its core.

Because that is what grief really is; not just an ending, not just sorrow, but devotion. A reminder that we loved, that we dared to care, that life is fragile and fleeting as it is still worth giving ourselves to with our whole hearts.

The voice of grief is such an individual one, and sometimes I wonder if it is a voice at all, or more often a lack of a voice we would love to hear again. Grief has its ways of speaking, but it also has its ways of withholding, of holding us still and in a wordless void.

When grief arrives, it often steals our words. We do not know what to say, or when to say it, or whether speaking at all will make the ache more real. Sometimes we fear that giving grief a voice will upset others, or reopen wounds that seem to have just begun to heal.

Sometimes we stay quiet out of fear of saying the wrong thing to a person that is grieving, or not being understood. I know I have swallowed countless sentences because I was afraid they might not land as I intended, especially as someone who had a night of grief turned into an excuse to say the most careless and hurtful things that no child should hear from anyone, let alone a parent.

I have sat with grief over and over and the only way we survive it is to greet it like an old friend who is a much faster runner than we are, because there is no escaping it. To live fully is to experience grief.

In my own losses, I have felt that silence pressing in. There were moments I wanted to speak on this and I found myself hesitating. Would others be uncomfortable? Would I reopen their wound? Would I reopen my wound? Would they think I was dwelling on something they wanted to leave behind? This fear creates a silence that can feel just as heavy as grief itself.

That is part of the paradox of grief; how desperately it longs for expression, and yet how impossible it can feel to let it out. And yet, the voice of grief also holds great power when we find the courage to use it. To speak of the ones we loved, to share their stories, to say their names aloud, this is one way grief transforms into devotion. When we give grief a voice, we give love a place to land. We keep memories alive. We let others know they are not alone.

But not every grief is meant to be spoken. Some griefs ask for quiet reverence, for the privacy of silence. Silence itself can be a language of respect, an honoring of the depth of what we feel. Sometimes words would only diminish the weight of it, and so we sit in stillness instead. I have learned to trust both the times when grief needs a voice, and the times when it asks me simply to listen.

This is part of what makes grief so mysterious. It does not have one voice, but many. Sometimes it wails, sometimes it whispers, sometimes it hides. Sometimes grief shows up in our bodies without our minds having a clue why. And always, whether in silence or in speech, grief is love trying to find its way through us.

That is why joy often comes tangled in its wake. Because in speaking or in staying quiet, in weeping or remembering, we are reminded that we cared. That we dared to love. That we have lived deeply enough to lose. And that is a gift we get to hold.

I spent a lot of my life trying to hold other people's grief – trying to lessen it, soften it, or somehow get it right. Whatever *getting it right* even means. The truth is, grief belongs to each individual to hold. And I think that's what the voice of grief ultimately teaches us: there is no perfect way to carry it, no perfect words to offer, no map to follow. Its an individual process that we can only try to support for those we love on both sides of the veil.

There will be times we cannot speak, and that is OK. There will be times we find the courage to give our grief a voice, and that too is sacred. What matters is that we honor it, however it chooses to come. For grief, whether in silence or sound, is always the echo of love.

THE SOUND OF FIRE

Journal entry —

I can't remember a time where I have been this embarrassed! Let's be honest, you probably could if given the time though Char.

I did the most insane thing today, I recorded my internal ranting out loud. I sent it to a friend as sort of a quickfire and quite careless accountability action. Told her she didn't have to listen, I just needed someone to know I am an arsehole, or perhaps I wanted someone to reassure me that I wasn't — wrapped in that much emotion we may never be entirely sure what I was thinking beyond white hot anger.

I'll give you the cliff notes because I listened once and was so horrified at my venom I deleted it. I ranted about the fact it's always me that notices, always me who checks in.

I can't not, I won't explain it more than that, it's done now and I don't want to expand on it. I will say it was as if someone had popped the lid off of a very deep well of emotions and I wasn't a fan of hearing it out loud. It made me feel shameful to say those things about a friend and then I started laughing at how hilarious I sound when fuelled by rage. I'd love to say I didn't recognise my voice, but I did.

Out of the window I just saw a sort of cloud-like curtain pull back very slowly to leave a patch of clear sky — I wouldn't have noticed if the edges weren't as sharp. Symbolic much.

I feel a little better. Silly almost, ashamed a little. But better, everything is clearer.

Cxx

Letting emotions move through you is very different to letting your anger fly out of you and become a weapon, though that is easier said than done at times. One brings release, the other destruction. During the days that followed I knew I had a choice, either to repeat what I had witnessed and become bitter, or to break the pattern and allow myself to feel the hurt without turning it into harm.

So I sat with it on the inside. I journalled it out and howled at the moon, letting the waves of grief and disappointment crash and recede until they softened into something else, something I could carry without it carrying me. Anger may have been the loudest voice at that time, but I was determined not to let it become the focus of my life or the only one I listened to. I am not defined by what was done to me, but by what I choose to do now.

The voice of anger is another that we think we know, and we often shut down when we hear. I remember the time my step-dad was screaming in the car for some reason and, I think, pulled over near a village where his friend lived. You know what though? I couldn't tell you the rest because my brain has taken that memory and locked it away somewhere safe so I don't have to relive it as an adult, let alone a child.

It's a well-known quote that when we start shouting, people stop listening and yet some clearly haven't received that memo. There is so much shouting in the world at the moment; too much maybe. I get that there is a need for people to stand up for what they believe in, I really do. And I know that using our voice is how we begin to create the change we need to see; yet when one group starts shouting, the others get louder in response until the spectators honestly have no clue what's going on and they often switch off.

Brene Brown once said: "Women are taught that anger is unladylike — that it makes us difficult, irrational or unlovable. But anger is a map and if we ignore it we get lost".

I can't help but wonder if there is a pattern here that becomes apparent when we hit menopause. All that bottled up rage just floats right to the surface and ripples through the skin until there is no way to avoid it. With this in mind, I attempted to befriend my anger often and to listen to her, not through fear but through a desire to understand what I'm feeling and why.

This sacred dance with rage means that firstly I can't walk off the metaphorical dancefloor because I simply don't like the song. It means I have to stay and listen; and what is often harder, I also have to stop myself from immediately texting a friend to validate my anger and immediately divide the burning sensation inside. I have to stand in all of it. I don't always manage that, but it can't be love and light all the time, can it? Sometimes I need to give my shadows a voice too, or they'll fester within.

If ancestry is the root that grounds us, lineage is the thread that carries us forward. Lineage weaves into the very fabric of our being, often unnoticed, like magic. And sometimes the threads that carry us forward are not the wounds but the smallest, quietest gestures.

For years I associated my blood lineage with anger and drama; one half of the family refused to speak to the other, there was backstabbing, bitter debates over "rights" to sit in funeral cars, brushes with illegality, and enough secrets to fill volumes. It was no picnic. Even though my willingness to dive deep into my own emotional wounds convinced me I could stop those ripples from reaching my children, what I hadn't recognised was that lineage runs deeper than a history of wounds or poor behaviour — and, more often than not, those hidden threads are the most luminous of all.

I realised this one day while peeling potatoes. Ashley asked me why I always peeled them in warm water and with that particular knife. The knife I could explain; it was my favourite. But the potatoes? I hadn't thought about it until that moment.

I pictured myself as a child, sitting on the draining board, peeling potatoes into murky water. My parents and grandparents had done it to clean them. I was doing it purely out of habit because I liked the warmth on my hands and because it kept the peel from scattering across the floor.

Do you see how simply lineage threads weave quietly in and out of our lives? Sometimes they are so small, we hardly even notice until someone asks the right question. Just like peeling potatoes in warm water, or never eating the end of a banana. These little habits are the fabric of lineage too, as much as surnames or traditions.

But lineage is not only what we inherit, it is also what we choose. For a long time, I thought I had to heal my grief before I could move forward, searching for an antidote that never came. Slowly, I learned the only way through was to live inside it. I curled up in the dark cave of myself and found, eventually, wildflowers growing on its walls. That cave of mourning became a womb-space of rebirth; my own version of a church.

It was there I began to wonder: what if joy could be my lineage? What if the thread I followed forward didn't need proof or pedigree, but simply had to feel true inside me?

Just as I had inherited patterns and behaviours from my ancestors, I was now becoming an ancestor myself, laying the groundwork for the generations that would follow on from my children. I felt a deep sense of responsibility, not just to heal myself but to heal the lines of women and men who had come before me and those who would walk this Earth after me.

I had always felt as though I had to carry all of my family's burdens; as if it were my job to hold the weight of every unspoken word, every misstep and every silence. But now, I was realising that lineage wasn't just about having what was passed down to me. It was about passing something forward. It was about releasing what no longer served me and gently weaving new patterns for the future. It was about allowing the web to slide through my fingers and keep moving forward.

The cave I had curled up in no longer felt like a tomb, it was a place of creation where I was forging the tools to carve a new path. As I began to look at my lineage with a new perspective, I realised that the old family stories — the ones that had once caused me pain — were not my prison.

They were threads in the fabric of my being, each one woven with wisdom and love, each one holding its place in the larger tapestry of life. I began to consider this disownment, as I called it, as a gift; something that finally made me sit up and see what I had known was always there: A better pathway for my family.

The letters I had written became the vessel to pass on weren't just letters. They were an invitation to step fully into my power, to embrace the joy of possibility, and to release the grief that had kept me tethered to the past. I was no longer just a product of my lineage. I was actively shaping it.

We are so often invited to carry forward our family's grief, yet we forget that grief can be a portal towards more joy. With joy, there is also grief.

From that day on, I began to see myself not as an individual alone but as part of a much larger web eternal circle of life and love. My ancestors weren't gone. They were with me, woven into every choice I made and every step I took. And now, I was part of the lineage that would one day guide future generations. Their joy, their pain, their wisdom, and their mistakes flowed through me, and I would carry them forward with curiosity, love, and an open heart.

It was then that I truly understood the frequency that pulls the inner cord. It's joy, yes, but it's also love; the deep, unshakable love that binds us to the land, to the sky, and to the stories passed down through the ages. And as I sat with my letter to myself, I realised that joy wasn't something to wait for, it was something to create. It was something to call forth with every breath; with every movement of my hands in warm water, with every word I spoke to myself, and every action I took toward healing.

The day I walked to the nursery to pick up Theo, headphones on full volume, and was able to sing the bridge of Paramore's *Ain't It Fun* without crying, I knew I was moving in the right direction. Joy was calling my name, and now I could not only feel it more deeply and appreciate the preciousness of it, but I could hear it guiding me to better things. Things that excited me, things that I couldn't explain quite yet but I could feel them bubbling away under the surface.

Heart Thread – Each of us holds multiple threads of lineage. They go way beyond our DNA no matter the circumstances or happenings of how we got to this moment. There is a profound and powerful story of lineage woven in there somewhere, I promise you. Sometimes it might feel as if that has skipped a generation or two, but deep down within you, there is always a thread just waiting for you to tug on it from the ground and continue to walk forward with it.

I started to notice joy in all its forms; In music that carried me from grief into release, in the rebellious colours of Banksy's street art that reminded me of freedom, in learning to crochet square by imperfect square, even in mistakes that became their own kind of offering. I began to think maybe mistakes themselves were lineage too.

Joy became not something frivolous but something ancestral. A thread I remembered from childhood, a thread that felt like my own contribution to the long weaving.

Lineage, I realised, is not only what we are given, it is what we decide to cultivate and carry. And if I have the choice, I will always choose joy.

THE MELODY OF JOY

If grief has a voice, then so too does joy. Where grief is often hushed, tentative, and carried in silence, joy tends to sing, even if only softly at first. And yet, I have learned that the two are not opposites, they are bound together. Joy is made sharper by grief; it shines more brightly because of the shadows we have walked through.

For a long time, I thought joy had to be loud and obvious: big belly laughs, wide smiles, sparkling moments of celebration. But the more I live, the more I notice that joy often speaks in whispers. It arrives quietly, almost shyly, in small moments that many would overlook: the warmth of sunlight on my face, the smell of coffee in the morning, a conversation with someone I love that leaves me lighter than I was before. Joy doesn't always announce itself; sometimes it simply lingers at the edges, waiting for us to notice.

And yet, joy also has a boldness to it. It is the laughter that bursts out in the middle of a heavy day and the relief of release after long-held tears. It is the moment you realise you are still capable of delight even after you thought you'd forgotten how. Joy surprises us, interrupts us, catches us off guard.

What I hadn't seen coming though, was the guilt I would sometimes feel for sharing my joy, even with those that want nothing more than to see me succeed. As if joy were something selfish; something indulgent that I should hold back out of consideration for the pain in the world or the struggle of friends. I have caught myself many times over the years dimming my own light so as not to cast a further shadow on someone else's sadness.

But I have come to realise that joy, when spoken aloud, is not a weapon but an offering. To voice our joy does not diminish another's grief; it can become a hand extended, a reminder that even in the darkest times there are still glimpses of beauty worth reaching for. Joy does not erase suffering, it sits beside it, whispering that life is still unfolding and still holding moments of grace.

I often think of joy as the body's way of remembering what it means to be alive. Where grief presses inward, joy expands outward. It makes space inside us. It stretches us open to possibility. And, like grief, it is not always easy to voice. Sometimes we withhold our joy because we fear it might seem foolish, inappropriate, or too much. Sometimes we hide it because others are grieving, and we worry our joy will sting them. Just as grief silences us out of fear of saying the wrong thing, joy too can be muted by self-consciousness.

But when we give joy a voice; when we let it be seen, heard, and shared in any environment — not selfishly or without consideration — it multiplies. Joy is contagious. One person's laughter can ripple through a room, loosening what is heavy. One expression of wonder can remind us all to look again, to notice what we missed. Joy's voice is not meant to be hoarded, it is meant to be offered over and over again, in the small ways and the big.

Some of my deepest experiences of joy have arrived right alongside grief. It seems almost irreverent, but there it is the laughter at a funeral when a story is told that perfectly captures the spirit of the one we've lost.

The sudden wave of gratitude for snuggles in bed with your children in the middle of mourning, when I realise how lucky I was to have loved someone so deeply. Joy often threads its way into the very heart of sorrow, reminding me that loss is only possible because love was here first.

Like grief, joy wears many faces. Sometimes it is exuberant and uncontainable. Sometimes it is quiet and private, something we hold close inside. Sometimes it is found in company, other times only in solitude. There is no single way to name joy, no single voice.

What I know so far is this joy is a gift, and like all gifts, it asks to be received. It does not demand we earn it, nor does it wait for our lives to be perfect before it arrives. It comes in flashes, in glimpses, in unexpected moments of grace. And we must try to notice it when it comes. Honor it by speaking it aloud, by letting yourself laugh without apology, by saying thank you for even the smallest pleasures. I try to let joy be a teacher, just as grief has been.

Joy is not only found, it is also made. We get to notice it, create it, nurture it, and choose how it shows up in our lives.

If grief is the echo of love, then joy is love in motion. And we give joy a voice when we let it flow through us — we not only remind ourselves how to live, but we give others permission to do the same.

THE SUPPORT BENEATH MY FEET

The support I needed, I found in the land. This continued for weeks on end. I would take the children to school, go home, peg out the washing, make a flask, and just walk with the dog until we found a spot to sit and rest. The resistance to not offload slowly slipped away, and the more I shared, the deeper I felt myself slip into the land's embrace.

I began to tell the land my stories and sing songs. It felt a little silly at first, hidden under the silver birch around the edges of the wildlife park behind our house, dog at my feet. In my daily confessional, I stumbled over my words and sobbed until I shook over what I had thought to be random chapters of my life. All the while, it felt as if the land just wanted to be there with me in silence and consistency. Sometimes, she would send a bird to the tree, and other times she would send me a warm breeze to acknowledge she was listening and I was heard.

Each day, never knowing what story would float to the surface, I told her how tired I was; how exhausted I felt in my bones, and how many times I felt torn between saving the world and burning it to ash. I sang her songs and she sent me birds to sing back a reminder that the world itself carries voice. I laughed at myself, and I'm sure she laughed too when I came to the realisation that I didn't want to be a princess locked in a tower, but I also didn't want to be the one saving everyone either.

I cried until my eyes became so puffy I would force myself to stop, run home to splash cold water on my face, feed the dog, and quickly reply to my client emails before picking the children up again. I shared my shame in my silence and my words, and I listened for the response in my body to the words that flowed from my mouth day after day after day, until I was done. The tears stopped and for the first time in my life, I felt empty and not in a numb way, but in the best kind of way.

I felt as if all of the layers of me had unravelled through the summer, and by autumn, all I felt was a deep grief for my children, even when I knew that grief is teaching us back to a deeper version of love. They had lost an entire section of their family tree that I wasn't sure was wise for them to reclaim. I searched high and low for what little I had in my memory of my grandparents, what I knew of my great-grandparents.

I watched other people's families, and at one point, I wasn't sure I would ever find the feeling of that golden connectedness of all again. I would see them sharing their lives through all phases, and though I do not carry a single drop of regret for walking the path that led me here, still something was missing. I felt as if I was walking on automatic; I just moved through each day and was not really in my body, as if some part of me had yet to return and root into what my daily life was.

To the outside world, I imagine I looked like my usual self. That or I was burning so hot that no one dared ask how I actually was. I often wonder what it's like when the strong one crumbles in front of you. I don't think I've seen it, because I am usually the strong one. I was the one everyone turned to, and yet on the inside, I was equal parts hollow and heavy.

More than a year had passed and winter had come and gone again. I was walking through the cherry blossom near my home when I was shown a very different type of forest. I saw myself on my knees, with my forehead pressed to the bark of a giant, rather gnarly-looking tree that was unlike anything I had ever seen in real life before.

I watched myself sob, whilst holding this tree, and every part of me wished I could let go; take a knife, cut a branch, and together we could replant our tree and feed it with love. I told this version of myself that we could dig the new hole together, pick the perfect spot, I promised. She shook her head between sobs until I sat with her and placed my hands on that very same tree to see what she could see that I was missing.

I watched every family moment I could remember and beyond flash behind my eyelids. The good: my nan's quick wit, my grandad's cheeky laugh, playing with coppers while watching the horse racing, singing to Neil Diamond and Roy Orbison in the back of my dad's Mondeo, the smell of freshly made jam tarts, making wine glasses from Cadbury Rose sweet wrappers at Christmas, licking a red Smartie and rubbing it on my lips to look like lipstick with Aunties, Swan oven hob toppers and red and cream flock wall paper; walks in the forest at Easter, the smell of my brother's train track, and my very first desk.

They flew through my senses and on the wind until I felt them step behind me: my ancestors. My Nanny Pat and her mum, babies, I can only assume I was never told about or ones that I never got to meet. I saw the Tanners, the Patricks, the Haycoxes, the Pearces, and beyond the names I knew. Realising that, more often than not, the things we see as a curse are often the deepest blessing.

And I knew. Right then, I knew. There was more good in this family tree than bad. We try so hard to believe we can sever ourselves or someone else from our ancestors. I thought not only of my own experiences, but of all the people I had met through workshops and events who didn't feel as if they had an ancestral leg to stand on. Who was I to think that a couple of people in my ancestry could decide to cut me off? Only I had that power, and I chose to stay. Staying doesn't always mean going backwards.

Journal Entry — Summer 2021

Really strange dreams the last two nights. Those ones where you aren't fully awake and navigating the outcome, but more observing the unfolding in a sort of semi conscious state.

I revisited the people from my past and I chose to go back with them. I quit jobs, I moved towns and gave up homes only to later realise the person I had returned to hadn't changed. It was the strangest thing to sit there and feel this understanding in my body.

The realisation and the drop of my stomach, I was disappointed for them and a little for me. The last two nights this has happened in so much detail. The smaller things I wouldn't have noticed back then coming into clear sight through a dream. Even when I woke up and went back to sleep several times, the dream returned exactly as it was before and continued.

Thank you for showing me this. I have felt so incredibly alone recently, well maybe most of my life to some degree. This has shown me how far I have come through the tears and sleepless nights. A sleep messenger reminding me of my growth, to forget about the past and to keep moving forward.

I belong exactly where I am and I am never alone. Cxx

I began to relook at the word ancestry and realised — no, remembered — that we are so much more than the two generations before us. Let's do some very rough ancestral maths here. In the space of just over four hundred years, you could have up to four thousand and ninety four ancestors across only twelve generations. Picture that on a web and remember we each get to choose which threads we pull from. Not all of them are going to make excellent decisions in life, and yet every single one of them carries wisdom down the line to us.

I believe ancestry is what holds us; it is wholly rooted in the Earth. Even when our family tree feels a little unstable in the thunderstorms of emotions, we must trust that in those roots, there is always good. And through all of the errors and misguided decisions of our ancestors, those glimmers of goodness are asking to be remembered.

Yet, it would be a great disservice not to acknowledge the lesser moments. We must claim it all; good and bad, loved and detested. Those family lines we would rather forget about run in our blood, and without acknowledging them, are allowed to hold a shadow of power over us.

I often talk about conversations with the land through my work and yet, for some, it might feel a little too out there to believe or see that the land is talking to us.

But it really does constantly talk to us all. The direction the coastal wind blows almost freezing the trees in a certain direction. The way flowers tell us what they need or how plants die back or change colour to symbolise the change of the seasons. It isn't always deep but the land does have a voice and it's one we often forget to include or discredit and unimportant compared to humanity's high demands.

Once I had sat in my grief for an entire cycle of the seasons, the land spoke and I was ready to listen.

I speak with the fire of miners and witches.
I speak with the water of oceans and grandmothers' tears.
I speak with the wind that howled through factory gates and coastal caverns.
I speak with the stone – old, unyielding, sacred.

This voice is not new.
It is as ancient as the land that carries it.
As real as the soil beneath my feet, and the branches above my head.

I speak now –
Not for them,
But for me,
And for the ones who never got the chance.

THE LAND CLAIMS YOU AS HER OWN

Living in different places across the UK, a lot of people would ask me how we got here. It's the accent you see, people immediately notice "you aren't from around here" when you speak differently. I considered what it felt like when people made a comment about my accent, because I didn't think I had that much of an accent until our move to Yorkshire.

But, more than that, moving away from where we grew up gave us a chance to find a family voice of our own. Our own beliefs, our own traditions — not just talking about them, but having enough space to actually live them.

I remember looking at the uniform list for my daughter's new school in Yorkshire and wondering why they call a lunch box a 'pack-up', then having to search "sand shoes" online because I had no clue what they were. Turns out they are black daps — or that's what we called them in the South, maybe some people call them plimsols? There are numerous other language differences too, like being invited to a neighbour's house for a 'gab' (chat or a catch up) or when ordering a 'bread cake' instead of a 'bread roll'.

Not so long after moving North, I happened across a clip from the TV show *This Morning* with Josie Gibson and British actor James Purefoy.

Born in Taunton, James found himself tearful while listening to Josie speak, because you don't hear a West Country accent very often unless in the stereotypically negative way, and hearing it just in everyday conversation or, in this case, an interview made him feel happy and at home.

Watching this interview back, I was reminded of a time when my dad started work for Bristol City Council and his colleagues used to make snide comments about his accent. He quickly dropped his Bristolian tones, although I've seen them occasionally appear in frustration or joyous celebrations with his sisters. I considered what it felt like when people made a comment about my accent, I began to wonder when did we begin to see our accents as a label we were trying to avoid or even run from?

My daughter took on a Yorkshire accent at school as almost a performance, and a stellar one at that! Meanwhile, my son kept his Bristolian tones throughout. His nursery teacher even commented one day on how she loved the way he said her name 'Claire'. You can bet your bottom dollar he picked up all of the Rs that others had dropped and used them to their fullest.

My husband has a knack for accents, which was possibly ignited from his time in the military. He has been known to use a selected accent for an entire day just for fun in our house around Christmas time. One year, I had laughed so much that by lunchtime, I needed a nanna nap!

We Bristolians love our words. We laugh at ourselves and we love our R's. I often used to tell my children that in Yorkshire they drop letters, and in Bristol we sound as many as possible, sometimes adding in a few for luck or luv; primarily an 'r' sound on the end of words! It took me a while to get used to the Yorkshire accent; I once spent ten minutes looking for Essele Road in Hull, to realise that it was in fact 'Hessle' Road!

I have pondered this idea of accents and our use of language through many turnings of the wheel. From the times I stand at gymnastics and a parent says, " Ey, ur not from round ere, are ya?" to the times on the phone when I have given my address, and the comment has been that my accent doesn't match my postcode. I was once at the park and told by a parent that when they stopped at a service station in the South West, their child had said everyone sounded like me.

We can pretend that accent bias does not exist but let's be honest, it really does. I might slow my words a little in a recording to be understood and to find a little grace with what is coming through, but why is it we have been taught to believe that our accents make us lower class?

Does it work the same when someone with what the world would call a working-class accent on the train hears someone with a rather posh accent and vice versa? Do they immediately repel in opposite directions like magnets? Does one think, "I'm out of my depth with this posh guy"? Does the other somehow feel a little superior or as if they are better?

How did we begin to place shame on the fact that someone is so deeply connected to the land they were born part of that it is shared daily in the tones of their voice? And why,in those moments of extreme emotions, do our accents reappear as if the rage we sometimes feel pushes through so determinedly, or the joy explodes so quickly, that no amount of shame could mask the tones the land gifted upon us when we were born.

I can't help but wonder if we should begin to look at our accents as a gift and a skill, the same way we do when we hear someone speak a foreign language so fluently and beautifully. There is no shame in having an accent; each accent quite often uses a different part of the mouth with its individual rise and fall notes, all unconsciously learnt from the land and the people that raised us? How is this not seen as a magickal signet of belonging?

It is my belief that when we really strip it back to the bones of it, our accent was carved by the land from which we were born, and that in itself is a badge of honour we should wear with pride. I often imagine how the land we call home has shaped us in many ways; from our ideas of work, abundance, home and family. Yet there is something so powerful about your accent and the words you speak, being a part of the land that we need to remember. Yorkshire showed me this.

Here in Cornwall, for some reason, people cannot always understand what I am saying, which is fascinating considering I am not too far from where I grew up, really. So much so that I sometimes find myself speaking what a friend has called my 'National Trust voice' as it was first heard when I needed to request a car to take us back to a stately home.

I do it in situations where I want the person behind the desk or at the end of a phone to understand me clearly. Why? Possibly so I don't feel the shame of having to repeat myself. Or could it be that the Natty T has a certain type of member; a bit like a golf course members club? No shade here, just facts; some places bring out your telephone voice in person.

We can also pretend it doesn't make a difference, but it does. Only last week my husband needed an emergency dental appointment and he tried for days, until I said I would make some calls whilst he dragged himself into work. Let's just say my telephone voice struck gold. It could have been luck, or it could have been the fact my voice down the telephone line was more appealing than a grumpy man in pain. (sorry babe). It's wrong, but we all do it without realising, and that realisation is how we move forward and make change.

Another of my most recent realisations to add into the mix was the 'mum voice'. I apparently use this when checking in on people I care about. It's a lot higher than my normal speaking voice and I never knew it existed until I used it once with a friend on a weekend away and her response knocked me so hard I spent most of the weekend trying not to cry, and ensuring my voice stayed in its usual range. I didn't mean to upset anyone, I wasn't even aware it existed until I double checked with my children and they said they hadn't really noticed before.

Words matter. They always matter. But over-polishing them and rephrasing them makes them lose a certain potency. For weeks after this discovery I considered how often I was not only softening my words, but using the tone of my voice without realising. As per my usual style I beat myself up about it, until one morning I woke up and thought I was a child abandoned by her mother for her silence, and now my tone has to be a certain way?

We ALL do it one way or another. Some of us raise our voices to be heard, some of us over-pronounce our words because we were sent to schools to ensure we do so — because in turn that ensures we get the good jobs and the respect from our peers; others double down on their local tongue.

On our way to visit friends in the South West, we stopped off for food and a panic pee. The children had gone to look at the soft toys that we would inevitably have to try and squeeze into the car while I sat with my eyes closed and the Sun shining in from across the field.

That's when I heard it: two thick Bristolian accents from the table behind. They laughed and joked about their weekend plans, and I couldn't help but to sit in the comfort of the familiar sound of their voices — even if I didn't know them the love that I felt in the familiar tone was gurt lush. I felt as if their words had washed me in a sort of golden glow.

Sir Ian McKellen talked about a similar feeling once. He shared how when he gets into a taxi in Manchester at Piccadilly station and hears the driver say, "Where are you going to love?" He feels he is home in a place where grown strangers call each other love.

I knew what he meant right there in that service station ear-wigging over my coffee. The two women laughed and talked, about what I am unsure of.

It wasn't really the words I was tuning into; it was that comforting, familiar tone of home.

I often think the land grieves when we feel shame for our accents. There are so many ways that humanity is cutting itself from the land that our ancestors swore to protect. Our voices are only the beginning. Where we were born is a gift and we no longer live in a time where how we speak should be considered less than. It's easy to forget that, before we were enslaved by the rich men who 'owned' the land, we loved our accents and remembered we were moulded from the land itself.

Heart Thread — There is no perfect voice, there is no perfect pattern of speaking because every conversation is different. There is only acceptance. Every accent and every voice inside of us deserves to be heard and accepted. The angry, the quiet, the loud. Yup. All of them.

THE SILENCE THAT SPEAKS

There are seasons when language slips beyond my grasp when even music cannot carry me where I need to go. In those moments, sometimes in the void when the words are rising within we need to reach to a palette of tools much wider than speech.

When I ached to hold onto the smallest glimmer of my roots, I turned toward the work of Banksy. We would often speak of the day they climbed a fence and left their mark on the playground wall of my daughter's nursery, as though rebellion itself had brushed against the innocence of childhood. Even now, as I edit these words, Banksy has just placed a new piece on the Royal Courts of Justice — an act that feels like a reminder: art speaks where voices are silenced. I read books about their work, followed each post and, to this day, whenever a fresh Banksy appears, I know it is a good day for the rebels.

Art can be a voice that stands the test of time. Quietly remaining on the walls and speaking its message that often humanity would rather avoid or forget.

I am no painter by the world's standards, yet sometimes a brush finds its way into my hand. Colour spills where words cannot, symbols rise to the surface – shards of memory, whispers of the future, the unseen etched into form. But our stories are never confined to paper or canvas alone. They seep into every vessel willing to carry them.

I have learned that we are drawn to films and series not only for comfort, but for the way they pull emotions to the surface. Sometimes we need the permission of a story to weep. And often, it is not even the whole story but a fragment – a single line or a fleeting swell of music – that reaches inside and touches the ache we are not ready to name, or stirs a truth we do not yet understand.

My husband laughs at my love of deep-diving the symbolism in movies and programmes. For him, it is entertainment; for me, it is translation. During the darker months in my mind, I watched a lot of the series *Heartland*. Simple, consistent and loving. My mind and my body needed the visuals of the wide open spaces, the freedom of the horses and the love of a family. I wonder how often we find much deeper comfort in forms of media than we realise.

One Christmas I sent out emails and texts asking our friends and extended family for their favourite recipes. I was craving a tradition, something that felt similar to family; a connection maybe. We gathered a book of handwritten recipes and gave them to our daughter over the festive period. The book we still use today and for years to come. It has become a chorus of voices made edible, an inheritance of taste.

I've spent many a morning dancing in the kitchen letting what I do not have words for move through my body with my headphones on as the kettle boiled. I keep a grimoire of sorts where I cut out poems, pictures, oracle cards or postcards that express what I am craving or what is emerging from within. This is all a part of my voice, the who I was and the who I am becoming. You see, voices aren't only made of words. You know that by now, right?

Expression is not always found in the voice we own. Sometimes it is borrowed, sometimes stumbled upon, sometimes painted, filmed, or whispered back to us by others. And when the words are hard to reach, that too is a kind of language.

THE LIGHT I GAVE

“Don’t be so hard on yourself,” my husband said as we followed the winding lanes towards the ocean. “I know, but I messed up, and I should know better.” He squeezed my thigh as the stereo blasted out and, as per usual, I let the tears slide flow behind my sunglasses.

You know I never know what it is about cars; is it the fact it's a small space, or the fact that you are talking but the person isn’t looking at you directly? Maybe it's the music as well, I just always cry in cars. It could also be the possibility that life gets so busy that longer car journeys are the rare opportunity to dive a little deeper or fully catch up, I can never be sure.

For the longest time I have been my biggest critic. From the shame I carried over things I had taken that didn’t belong to me in 2010, to the over-sharing in a supermarket back in 1999. I’m not sure my over-analysing brain will ever fully give that up, but it has learnt to let a lot go. You see, in a world that constantly highlights our imperfections, I’m not sure the voice I heard often in the back of my mind was always either my own or helpful.

When you write a book, at some point through the process you take the concept of 'everyone has at least one book in them' literally and push everything onto the page out of fear that you will never get another chance. But also this is another voice thing, right?

We want to take the opportunity to be heard right to the edges of its capacity? We want everyone to hear every thought that has kept us up at night, every mistake we wished we could erase or apologise for. We want to free ourselves of the voices and also be free of *the voices*.

At some point during the writing process (forgive my lack of time awareness but it often becomes a blur in my mind), I began to see the layers peel back over and over again. Every edit was a voracious muddle of all the things I wanted to say to the world to begin with, as if I had lifted the lid on the cage of every frustration I had or wished I could speak aloud.

The second time around, I not only had to remove the bones of at least one book from within the flesh of this one, saved for another publishing date. I also had to bring back the fire to my words through the exuberance of over-editing.

Like a crystal that had been tumbled over and over, my words had lost their potency, becoming almost too smooth for the intention of this book. I had created a work of over-devotion and zero rebellion. I was so frustrated with myself for doing the exact thing that I had wanted to warn the world about; smoothing it all out to make it easier to swallow.

Which leads me perfectly to community; something I over devoted myself to for a long time.

As children we were taught that to be a good friend you had to always be available, you always needed to have the answer or a solution. You needed to be positive, honest, and always leave things better than they were when you arrived. And, most importantly, if you didn't have a lot of friends you had failed, because there is nothing more sad than a scene of a movie where no one turns up to your funeral.

I was the friend who would sit on the phone at eleven o'clock at night, listening to someone I hadn't heard from in six months cry about their boyfriend. I was the first to offer help, to pop the kettle on or drop off flowers. I would tell my children, "We just have to drop these flowers off, so they know we care." "It doesn't matter if it's raining cats and dogs and almost tea time; they just need to know they're in someone's thoughts," I would say to my kids as we nipped out before tea to walk across the village to drop a bunch a flowers on someone's doorstep, then rushed home before our evening schedule was ruined.

I also went through a stage of offering out my husband's help to the neighbourhood. He would look at people's cars on a weekend or cut someone's tree down in their garden on an evening after work and, like the true warrior that he is, he never questioned the requests. He might have rolled his eyes a little, but I ignored it (sorry Ash).

Over the years I have, in some way, assisted hundreds of people across thresholds in their lives; divorce, financial worries, business start-ups, marriage and money struggles, and relocations hundreds of miles across the country. Friendship, to me, has always been an honour and one we forget can change lives.

Why? Because deep down, somewhere under all the noise and one-liners I have always believed in community, I believed in friendship and I knew we were collaborative beings. But at what cost? What price was I willing to pay my children's mental health, my physical health?

Tupac once said: " Just because you lose me as a friend doesn't mean you gained me as an enemy. I'm bigger than that, I still wanna see you eat, just not at my table." The problem was not only that I had been inviting all the people to my table for more than twenty years, I was also giving away the food I needed to eat.

For quite a few years I was aggressively helpful, I would constantly offer possible solutions or suggestions. Because we aren't good friends if we let someone suffer, right? Wrong. It's a tightrope to balance that only adult friendship can show you.

I collected all the friends I could find. I helped people, supported them, encouraged them — often to my own detriment. But I had so many that my phone would constantly be going off. And yet, deep down, I knew that very few were supporting me the way I was supporting them.

I was using my words in the name of community and what more could anyone want from me? Somehow I had this notion that this role would make me not only a great friend but worthy of friendship in return.

I was beginning to become frustrated at brightening someone's light or being the vessel to plant a seed. I felt used and, quite frankly, hurt by humanity. Because over and over again it was me showing up to help and then people were leaving, just the way my younger self believed my father had. I felt as if my heart was being used as well as my voice. I knew that Source was using me to encourage others, to show up, to lead.

They weren't using me, not really — source was. The mistake I was making was not knowing when to leave but, more importantly, I wasn't using my energy for myself first; something I persisted with until I became unwell.

I've pushed my body to the limit. I would unconsciously pretend I was fine and then vomit from anxiety behind the scenes. I'd spend three days recovering from an event or an unsafe circle. Over and over again I would show up for everyone and push through my body's messages because, in my eyes, I refused to give up. Other people needed looking after but not me.

I got so sick we actually couldn't find out what was wrong with me because there seemed to be no pattern in it. My body was screaming and yet, on the outside, I was being praised for "fighting for those I loved". And, more often than not, those I was fighting for wouldn't check in on me once a month, let alone remember when my birthday was.

Was my devotion feeding my rebellion? Or was my rebellion feeding my devotion? Or was it both and they just needed to be rebalanced before I ended up in hospital? All I knew was my body was in a rebellion against my brain and I was given no choice but to change that.

I wondered, could the two co-exist in my life and within my body in some sort of harmonious exchange? Until, bed-bound with a pain that felt as if I was pinned down, I realised I hadn't ever considered what my life would feel like if rebellion and devotion worked together?

Was this fire of rebellion in my core overriding what I needed most: devotion to self?

I had spent more than a decade speaking for others, defending people and adjusting the course of uncomfortable rooms, yet I don't remember more than a handful of times where someone else had done the same for me. This wasn't something I necessarily wanted or even knew I needed. But to hear it once was enough, and it wasn't even something big. Later down the line, with one half of my family were never close and the other half having abandoned me, I began to consider my friends my family. From the outside looking in, that must have felt as much of an intense honour and possibly a lot of unspoken pressure.

Someone had upset me; been a little more than careless with my often ridiculously open heart and I was holding back tears waiting for the kettle to boil. I wasn't crying because I was hurt, I was crying because I couldn't find the right words and, for so long, I had prided myself on the standard of my words. From the other side of the kitchen I heard my husband say, "This is not acceptable babe, you try too hard for people who try so little." I winced at the weight of the truth as I felt drop into the pit of my stomach. All I could do was nod my head and focus my blurry eyes on the sugar waiting in my coffee cup. It wasn't anything I didn't already know, yet often we just need to hear the words for them to settle in our bodies.

I needed to seriously take a pause more often and ask myself what it was that I was really rebelling *against* and why? I found many uncomfortable truths in those first few weeks.

Firstly I noticed that often I would say things to prove a point in environments that were an incredible waste of time, with people who have no interest in changing or seeing another's point of view — a waste of valuable energy. I then realised that though my fire defended my truth, it also prevented others from sitting with the uncomfortable of theirs.

Heart Thread — Many people speak to fill a void, not necessarily to add value, and that can drown out more considered or vulnerable voices. When was the last time you listened, not just to respond, but to truly understand? We often think we *should* have something to say all the time, especially in times of crisis. Sometimes silence is not absence, but a necessary pause.

THE COMMUNITY OF FALSE CONNECTION

Self Devotion is rebellion for women in a world determined to keep the exhausted and busy.

I spent centuries using my voice for others, while no one realised how bone tired and broken I was. But also, I believed I was being a bitch time and time again, because that's what the world told me I was.

Once I accepted this was a key theme for all the previous versions of myself, the game changed. I began to speak for myself first.

We can be devoted to many things in the world, but often at the bottom of the list is ourselves. Why? Because we are told it's selfish. We devote ourselves to higher causes, deities and gods. But to bask in the boudoir of our own self-care, to devote not only our time and voices to ourselves? I'm not sure I even knew how.

I needed to start small, and to make it a habit that was easy for me to maintain. So I chose the food shop. Steady, don't get overexcited.

I noticed that I had a tendency to buy everything everyone else needed. I'd remember that the crisps had changed so my kids didn't like those anymore, or that my son was running low on smoothies. And yet, I would entirely forget about myself. When the realisation hit me at home unpacking, I'd blame the overly loud checkout operator who needed everyone to hear what she had for tea, or the bright unnatural lights that left me overwhelmed. Whatever the reason, the truth was simple: I wasn't making myself a priority.

How pathetic, I thought to myself. If this wasn't a pure example of where the majority of my energy and intention was going, I didn't know what was.

And of course, I'm not alone with this; far from it. Women are taught to put themselves last before we even know we're women. From the moment we are handed a dolly to care for, or praised for being "helpful" with our younger siblings, the pattern is laid down: your worth lies in service.

We are rewarded for sharing, for giving the bigger slice away, for quieting our needs so someone else can be comfortable. Later, it becomes instinct. You don't even notice the automatic reach for the smaller plate, the forgotten jumper on a cold day, the way you nod along when you'd rather scream. It is stitched into us so early that we mistake self-neglect for kindness, exhaustion for love. When actually If we turn up the volume of our voices, we must do it for ourselves first.

Journal Entry Day 20 —

How on earth am I ever going to rewire my brain to stop having the impulsive urge to leap across every room and support someone or give them a solution!?

It makes me itch. But why? I suppose the question isn't why, we know why (It is all I have ever known). The question is can I find compassion in words rather than bursting into action and rescue mode?

What does that even sound like? Compassion without savior? Is it saying less? Is it sitting in silence with a person? Is that a gift in itself? To allow silence, does it create the space for another voice to rise? I'll have to keep trying.

Char — You cannot keep giving the entirety of your life force to others. You are approaching a place of no return, this is why you started this. Stick to the plan, Keep your over-offering gob shut.

Cxx

I hated the idea of not speaking for others. It went against everything in my body; everything I had been told made you a good big sister or friend. Everything that women are told is community and service-based.

Could silence be serving the community in a deeper way? Or does silence begin as an inside job first? A familiar voice dropped in, cool and wise: "*Only when we have sat in our own silence can we feel comfortable to allow others to do the same.*"

As quickly as she was there, she was gone again. OK, silence, I thought. I've been punished for you before in the worst ways. What's the worst that can happen?

Did I need to separate my emotional response from the situations? Partly yes. But I also needed to find a new version of empathy. A more verbal one that says " This sounds awful, I am here for you" instead of my usual "This is awful let me fix it!"

I started by stepping back a little from checking in on people. Not everyone, just the outer groups of people. If you imagine a web of spidey senses, or a network of other people's emotions with me in the middle, I just kind of called that web back toward me and inward.

Then when people messaged me, I didn't immediately respond to help them find a solution. I didn't ignore them either, I had empathy and I held space. But for the first time in my entire life, I no longer had unlimited energy for people to access; I came first.

And that meant people left. Again. My inbox got quiet.

I realised my circle was still too big. There was too much energy, too many family dramas, too many people sliding into my inbox only when they needed advice or help and, because I've never been someone who only commits fifty percent of her energy, I was all in. And this led me to feel empty and, quite honestly, unfulfilled. It wasn't that everyone was draining me intentionally; many people didn't even consider asking how I was or if I had the space mentally for them to unload their thoughts and struggles in my energy field.

The next layer for me was to put my little family before anyone in the hope I didn't make the shift too late and my children would learn, if only from my mistakes. And how did we get here, I wonder? Because it sounds almost insane to put anyone before your own household. And yet every series we watch, so many books we love – especially as women – are centred around the heart of a community. We often raise our daughters to give more than they receive with few boundaries until it's too late.

So I began to delay responses, I didn't reach for my phone as soon as it went off; in fact I switched off large amounts of notifications entirely, reminding myself that, in an emergency, someone will call or turn up on the doorstep. By applying these very small and silent changes to my everyday life, people drifted off from the fringes of my friendship circles. Immediate-response-Charlie was no longer available and, slowly, another chunk of my energy returned to me.

I also stopped over-offering to do things for people once I realised that, in doing so, I was trying to control the situation. I could see the possible outcomes and I wanted better for the other person, so I would continuously offer ideas, support, and tools.

I gave myself the rule of twice. I would offer to, I don't know, babysit because a friend says she and her husband haven't had a date night in years and really need to reconnect. I offer on the spot and she declines with something like, "Ah thank you for the offer," then changes the subject. Sometimes I'll follow up with a text later that week to say the offer still stands, or maybe it will come up again the next time we see each other. But after that second offer, I step back and let them decide. I'm not saying I would refuse if that friend came back to me months later and asked if the offer was still available; of course I would do it. What I am saying is that it's important to support others for their benefit, not as a control method for our own comfort or for their success.

People noticed and people noticed fast! And what happened next left me a little wounded: *they* vanished. After the mental adjustment of this and a bit of crying, I took all my energy back from everyone except my family. And you know what happened? Ninety percent of the people slipped away.

I don't say that in anger or as a 'poor me' tale, I tell you because it amazes me how far people drift without a second thought when we stop over-giving our energy. Did it hurt? Yes of course, and yet I kept reminding myself of two things: firstly my children were watching and I wanted them to never sacrifice too much of themselves for friendship and secondly, that self-devotion is not turning your back on others; it is the foundation that makes any true connection possible. Without it, you give from an empty cup. With it, you finally understand: love that doesn't include yourself isn't love at all.

Once I saw that my inability to let others figure it out for themselves was preventing their growth, whilst at the same time distracting me from my own, I wondered how I'd missed it before. But how many times, as the oldest daughter, was I encouraged to help the younger ones? How many times was I praised for looking after someone else?

Like a lot of deep healing, this process shrank my circle. It's often the way – we shed layers of ourselves and people vanish in the process. Some might call it a vibrational shift, but when you're in the thick of it, it just feels really crappy. Ghosting or silent treatment may be punishing you but it isn't about you, it's about the fact that that person cannot have a conversation that is a little difficult. So instead, they punish you with silence, hoping you'll either approach them and open up the awkward conversation or you'll leave them alone and the unspoken remains, well, unspoken.

I looked around and realised with our family returning to the South, we had a very small almost non-existent circle. It's amazing how relocation can reduce people's effort to stay in touch to zero quite literally overnight. But if I was going to reopen my doors to friendship — reluctantly I might add — then I wanted friends who met me where I was. Friends who weren't just showing up for their own joy so I had to play entertainer and who also had discernment, so I didn't have to slip into the role of protector. We needed a true sense of community.

Heart Thread — Self-devotion is not selfishness, it is rebellion. In a world that grooms women from birth to equate worth with service, the quiet act of choosing ourselves first is nothing short of radical. We are handed dolls and told to nurture, praised for shrinking our needs, rewarded for exhaustion disguised as love. And so we grow into women who forget that our bodies, our voices, our energy, were ever meant to be ours.

But here's the truth: when you stop pouring yourself out for everyone else, when you let silence settle and resist the urge to rescue, you don't just reclaim your energy — you reclaim your life. Circles shrink, yes. People fall away. But what remains is honest, sustainable, and rooted in reciprocity.

External voices of community are constant. We are trained to react, respond or post, but not to listen deeply. Speaking to be seen versus speaking to be understood, or to understand ourselves. The dominance of reaction culture (comments, quote tweets, "hot takes"), over reflection or dialogue means often fill conversations with words, yet somehow never really listen.

The biggest and most recent marker of this for me was at a dinner party. Firstly, I am not a dinner party fan if I'm honest; I'm more of a take away and a bottle of wine, or a home cooked meal around the kitchen table woman. The part that makes me itch is this idea that everyone *we* love is going to get on with *each other*; that always confuses me. But we made a promise when we moved to Cornwall to push ourselves so off we went.

Within the first half an hour I watched my very new friend accosted into a heated debate. I listened from the sofa next to my husband, firstly wondering how we got here. Was this why I didn't like dinner parties? I then watched the others in our group react to various levels of discomfort until I felt that feeling in my stomach and declared out loud that the conversation was giving me anxiety, so I was going to get a refill. No one else moved.

I came back five minutes later and the topic seemed to have changed but the energy was still a little too much for people who had just met, so I turned around and went back to sit at the table.

That night in bed, as we discussed the events of the evening, my husband declared that I left them all when those two people were in a heated conversation. I laughed as I pulled out my journal. "The rest of you didn't have to continue to sit there and listen, for me it feels like a big personal growth babe," I said.

For the first time in my life, I had left someone to defend themselves with zero guilt. I knew my new friend could defend herself – it's one of the things I admire about her. But still, there is something bigger than that we need to remember from this story, especially as women or as first-born daughters. For the first time I put myself first, and not in a silent way; I didn't stay in the room and shuffle in my seat. I stood up, explained my feelings with no expectation of change and walked away. It might actually be the very first time I didn't consider anything outside of my own feelings. Sometimes, the greater kindness is to let people sit in their problems and watch from a distance rather than pull them out with your own strength. It could be a debate, it could be a mindset hurdle or something deeper. By allowing them to climb out of the hole themselves, you give them the opportunity to dig deeper for a part of themselves they had forgotten existed.

Does it mean we leave our friends? Absolutely not. We sit with them, we take a step back and remind them they are strong enough to figure it out. The longer my friendship journey goes on, the more I learn. That's the joy and the struggle of it I suppose.

The balance of this is ever changing. I'll protect someone from a situation that presents real danger nowadays, but if you continue to return to the environment that is a wound for you then, without shame, I say that lesson is for you to learn and not for me to fix. I will always believe in the power of community, but not to the detriment of my own health

As we witness the generations coming up behind us and building newer, more inclusive versions of community, I simply hope they hold onto their voices and make their own needs a priority.

Heart Thread — I have always had an impulsive knee jerk reaction to protecting people. Call it human nature or plain, old-fashioned oldest daughter trauma, but this single thing was possibly one of the hardest threads to unpick from my personal pattern in life. The problem is two-fold;. firstly, I was so protective of other people that I began to resent it — after all, no one ever thinks to check if the louder people need defending. Secondly, I was preventing other people from learning to defend themselves. The voice of the community takes trust and discernment. It's never about fully solving each other's problems or putting your friend entirely before yourself. Never.

What is real community?

The word 'community' comes from the Latin communitas, meaning 'the same' and derived from 'communis', meaning 'shared.' That's what I needed; something shared, something real.

It's a community that sustains and nurtures us, holding us at every evolution of who we are and who we want to be. The problem is that as soon as we hear the word 'community' we think we must all agree on everything. If we don't, then we will feel triggered and all end up arguing, which isn't what those searching for a community want at all.

I am someone who has spent much of her life building what I could only describe as a solid community and network of souls who love me and mine. Do we all have the same opinion? No. Do we all have the same values? Yes, but we each work and live very differently. That is a true community; a group of people who return to love, even when they don't agree on everything.

True community is not found where we are pushed together in pews because we all want to be forgiven for our sins, or where we force opinions and beliefs onto others. Community doesn't speak for you. It listens and, if we are being honest, maybe it does judge, but it sits with that judgment and processes it rather than casting it out.

THE BEAUTY OF BEING WRONG

I mispronounce things so often I'm surprised my family hasn't nicknamed me Schmidt already. I use words in the wrong place, I can't spell very well and my grammar is often non-existent. I highlight words in my books like Josh Hartnett taught me as a teenager, so I can look them up later. I still get words wrong in all the ways, but this doesn't stop me; I choose to try and try again with words, just as I do with life.

Sometimes we get words wrong, it will happen. In haste, in carelessness, or fear. Sometimes it's simply that the listener didn't ask for clarification and totally misunderstood. I have, many times, chosen my words carelessly or with little thought and sometimes this has left me on the receiving end of silence.

Around 2022 I found myself on the receiving end of almost total silence for weeks, because I had made a poor choice of words. I had kept my sentence short and naively trusted that everyone in the room would understand what I meant. Epic fail on my part, because as truth would have it I really should have known better. Instead of my words being received the way they were intended, I was blindsided the following day by an accusation that I was behaving like a bully in the playground.

With my abandonment scar only just beginning to fade, I found it all of a sudden a much wider and nasty-looking open wound again. I returned to the downward spiral, this time not for my lack of words, but for my poor choice of them. I held my hands up like a big girl and owned how it had made people feel, but I also defended what I had said with honour; because my words may have been found lacking, but the truth of the matter remained and I felt it in my core.

Within a week I was starting to believe everything that was said about me. Silence is not something I'm afraid of – I actually adore the quiet – but a silence cast upon you by others hits differently. I burrowed into my little life wondering if there was any point in coming to the surface of the world again.

I replayed every single time I had made a poor choice of words and regretted it, every time I had lain in bed and played out a conversation I intended on having in the morning only to get it all jumbled in thoughts and air, every time I made a fool of myself with a boss, or carelessly outed a college friend.

When I began to speak again, I found the new scar had left me hyper-conscious of the words I chose. In many ways, I became fluent in the language of apology before I'd even said anything, or I would begin with things such as: "I just want to preface this by saying," or "I only say this because..." Or worse, I would use a word and then something in my body would panic and ask out loud, "Is that the right word?" By doing this, I was doubting myself and handing over the keys for sentence scrutiny to any and every listener.

Sometimes we're not just speaking to the person in front of us, we're speaking to all their past hurts; even if we don't know it. Looking back, it appeared the universe was determined to give me these examples in all of the ways. Shamed for speaking, cast out for not; over and over the cycle kept floating to the surface until I decided it didn't matter, not because it stopped hurting, but because I refused to let fear have a louder voice than my own any more.

I realised I was living in fear of a sentence that had already ended. Think about that; how often we give old words the power to shape our present selves. We will use the wrong words from time to time, we can open our mouths in the height of an emotion or select the wrong phrasing. Even text messages can be easily misinterpreted, because there is no tone, only words being read through our personal tinted glasses of life and past trauma.

Does that mean we should stop trying to communicate? NO. It actually means we are ALL being vulnerable in the present moment, and that has a forgotten power. It may also need a little extra pause and some grace added into the mix, but there is still power in our words, even when they are a little messy. There's something deeply human about fumbling through our feelings. I have had some of my most powerful and life-changing conversations through cracked voices and snotty tears as I've grabbed single words between gasps of air. Messy words don't always mean broken meaning.

You want to know the difference, don't you? You might think only a mad woman would say you have permission to let your words out, even when they're not perfectly edited. But I'm not asking for recklessness. I'm asking for presence, honesty, and care because you are casting words out into the world and those words are spells.

After months of sitting with every word I've ever replayed, I realised something, and I'll use myself as the example here, because that's all I've got. My intention has never been to purposely upset anyone, not ever. My intention has always been to change something, to improve it, to support or defend. And yes, I hear you; I was young, I didn't know any better. We both know this by now.

But here's what I've learned: intention only gets you so far. You can mean well and still cause harm. Intention can't be used as a shield to block, or an excuse for the aftermath, that's not how it works. Words live outside of us once they're spoken, and they land where they land. If they land heavy, if they bruise, that bruise is real whether or not you meant it. The work, then, is not to hide behind what you intended, but to accept the impact and decide what you'll do next. Remembering that if we never make mistakes, if we are never wrong, we never learn.

Then there's the pause. I can't overstate how much difference a single beat makes. One breath, one small silence between the thought and the release. That pause doesn't snuff out the truth, it roots it. It keeps your words from flying out white-hot and half-shaped, and instead lets them arrive steady, clear, rooted in clarity rather than reaction, and grounded in care not just release. I've learned that my words don't need to be quicker than the moment, they need to belong to it.

Another thing: listening. Not listening so you can jump in with your answer, or listening as a form of waiting, but listening long enough that you might actually be changed by what you've heard. That kind of listening alters the way words come out of you next. It stops them being echoes of your own voice and makes them part of a conversation, something shared.

And maybe this is the hardest piece; to remember that words can be carried like tools or wielded like weapons. The same sentence can mend or destroy depending on how it's held. The real question before speaking isn't, "am I right?" but, "what will this build, and what will it break?" Sometimes we think we're being honest when really we're being sharp, and sometimes we mistake bluntness for clarity. But sharpness cuts, while clarity opens.

When we do get it wrong – and we will – we have to be willing to go back. To return, to repair. A conversation doesn't end with the first draft of what we say. It deserves revision; we deserve revision. There's no shame in rewriting ourselves in real time. That’s the only way we grow into better keepers of our own voices.

When we choose this way with words, intertwining both rebellion and devotion, it's not always smooth, it's not always eloquent, but it's honest, and it lands.

THE TRUTH INSIDE THE TREMBLE

The more I began to share how I actually felt, having climbed through a very long phase of justifying why I was sharing or what I was saying, I noticed a new pattern: I had vulnerability hangovers that sometimes lasted for days.

In woo-woo work, we would call it an energy or magick hangover, but what is it in voice work? That period of time when you have dropped your walls and shared from a space of vulnerability. I've seen it in circles, I've felt it at events and in homes; not a performance come-down after a high, nor those reflections when you worry you might have overshared with someone. Let me be clear here, I'm talking about when you become a very raw version of yourself and the feeling afterwards can leave you feeling as if you have been cracked open and left in a heap on the floor.

You know those times when you have been so vulnerable, you've spoken through snotty gasps of air, hands quivering, and have said the words that have been building inside you? Not necessarily from a fire of rage and destruction, but from the silent and often shamed spark of needing more. I wish someone had reminded me of this when I began to return to speaking my truth.

Sometimes it's that you need more space, more time, more consideration, but more often than not it's that you need to be heard and your words acknowledged. This can happen in small ways, where you have to be honest with your boss or friend; you share how you feel, you sleep it off and your nervous system resets.

I began to see that the less I explained myself, the deeper my voice was rooting into my beliefs and my needs. This lack of sharing the "why" though often left me firstly with quite a gap of silence as the penny dropped from my share and then it also left me with additional questions: Why did I need that today? Why did I share that with that person?

I didn't always have the answers to those questions, only a desire to accept them as the person listening had. If given too much time to contemplate my actions I would quite easily end up back on the downward spiral of "I'm a bad person, I don't deserve to put myself first or prioritise my needs."

Then there are the bigger moments of vulnerability; I've had a few of these. The most recent one I can share was back in 2021. I was at a camping event when the host of the event decided that our little corner of the field had not contributed to the morning meeting as per her instruction.

Rather than her coming directly to us and speaking about the minor issue which, I might add, could have been easily explained, she thought it best to tell everyone on her way up towards our circle of tents what her intention was. She did this in such a loud manner that myself and the two men sitting around the fire heard every word.

I'm not sure if she was attempting to assert dominance as she got closer, or if she underestimated the carry of her voice, but by the time she got to the top of the hill I was ready. I let her say her piece and then I responded. The details aren't important here, besides the fact she was unprofessional as an event host and that, when she had the facts, we had done nothing wrong. It's the aftermath I want to talk about.

What followed were a couple of days of whispers from other camp members. I chose to keep my head down because my nervous system was shot. I felt as if I was on someone else's patch and whereas you would usually say your piece and walk away, I couldn't. So I put on a brave face, continued to show up around the campfire and then, when the Sun went down I'd throw my bundle of herbs on the fire and walk up through the dewy grass to the stone circle to sob. Something inside of me was breaking open and nothing – nothing – could stop it.

During our final full day on the campsite It was mentioned by several different people that they had heard about my 'speaking up' I smiled as best I could, mouth covered in cold sores (a common sign of stress and expressed high emotions) and sunglasses on to shade my swollen eyes, then I walked back to what I considered my safe zone; the circle of friends, where someone commented something along the lines of, "I'm so glad you said it on behalf of us all, because we were all thinking it." Bitterly, from nowhere, I replied, "Well if something needs to be said, I'm usually the one that says it, aren't I?"

I was done. I was sick to my back teeth of people letting me fight for them, letting me speak for them. What's more, I was more than a little ticked off that two men witnessed me have this altercation with the event host, when they could have ended the heat of it all with a couple of sentences. I felt unprotected as per usual, and wondered why not a single person besides my husband had asked if I was OK.

And I don't mean "How did you sleep?" I mean a real eye-contact question of "How are you feeling?" My tongue felt as if it was swollen and blocking my throat so I picked up my water bottle and a blanket, and walked behind my friend's truck to sit near the hedgerow of birds and try to find some sort of centre.

My body cracked as I lay on my side in the fetal position, at which point my friend Emma appeared and, in shock, said, “Oh my god, I thought you were OK with all this!” Another friend appeared with her daughter and, sitting there on the grass, I tried to explain the feeling.

I will fight for someone I love and I will always defend what is morally right; it's how I am wired, but that doesn’t mean I’m not exhausted or that my body doesn’t need a few days to recover, integrate and adjust to its new level. They nodded, there were lots of hugs and, that final night I walked up to the stone circle, sat with my back against the not so ancient rocks and I asked:

“What happens if everyone uses their true voice?”

“The world will change for the better,” I heard.

But it didn’t help me at the moment. I felt vulnerable and unsafe as my body adjusted to the fact it was now free of the words I had held back so many times. I wasn’t speaking just for me in this case, which brought the frustration, I was speaking for my camp mates and possibly every other soul who had been railroaded or crushed by the leader of camp who took a ‘my way or the highway’ approach.

Truth be told, I have had a few more of these moments, although possibly less dramatic. After a year of writing this book, I always thought it was pretty firy, but according to my editor — who knows me better than most — I was holding back. The question for myself was, why?

Was it because I didn’t want to appear that I was still a loose cannon? Was it that I still had a fragment of a fear of being completely seen? Or was it that I had spent so long with my own thoughts that I had somehow tumbled them around in my mind until they were smooth and shiny, like crystals that had lost their rawness; chapters all gleaming and lined up in a perfectly smooth row?

The instruction was to "get more emotional". Not to worry about the grammar and spelling (good job really) and to get all my frustrations and rants onto a page without reason or poetic rhyme, just as I had done in a journal for the past thirty years. The back and fourths of messages during that day of doubts reminded me of a song titled *If You Could See Me Now* by The Script. There is a line in the song (which is in the book playlist on Spotify if you haven't heard it) that says, "Take that rage, put it on a page, take the page to the stage and blow the roof off the place."

I played that song on repeat for two days; I typed and cried, cried and typed. I considered every time I had spoken up for someone else and every time I had said, "We don't do that here."

It turns out the fire was still there, I simply needed a reminder that devotion did not mean we entirely distinguish our fire and that I wasn't simply writing to empty myself of unspoken words. This book had a bigger purpose now I persisted, and I am so glad I did because I have not only written this book with every part of my heart, I have lived it.

Heart Thread – When you speak your truth, this often comes hand in hand with feelings of vulnerability. It will pass, your body just needs a little time to catch up and redistribute energy into the space you created by freeing yourself of the words you had been clinging to. There is no trick here, but I do find telling those closest to you that you feel vulnerable and need some space or time does help. And it is less likely you will storm off and have a breakdown behind your friend's truck.

THE OATH I MADE INTO AIR

In 2022 I stumbled out of bed to the familiar cry of the owls across the field. Sleep still hung heavy in my eyes, but there was something about the early morning that felt different today. With a quiet sigh, I slipped out of bed, found my favorite flip-flops, and padded toward the kettle with my journal tucked under my arm.

As I clicked open my in-laws' front door and locked it behind me, I walked the familiar footpath toward the water; barely a trickle of a stream now, barely an echo of what it once was. The land felt different, as though it, too, was changing, evolving alongside me. Through the low-hanging branches, I passed by, nodding to the trees that had witnessed so many versions of me. I made my way back to the bench I had befriended over the last few days, settling there with my mug clutched tightly in both hands.

Cornwall has always been more than just a place for me. It was a space that called to something deep inside me — something wild, untamed, full of possibility. I had made a secret promise to my ten-year-old self that one day, I would live here. It felt impossible then, a distant dream, something buried beneath the weight of years. But today, that dream was alive in my chest. And it felt like a promise kept.

Later that very morning we found ourselves in the same little fishing village where I had spent my summers as a child. I would rush out after breakfast in my pink jelly sandals to see what treasure the tide had brought in, and play until the Sun went down or until the fishing boats came and showed us their daily catch. It seemed like a simple enough day of sharing these memories with my family. Walking the winding coastal paths, standing on the lugger, watching the tide and buying ice cream; but it was more than that. There was a quiet magic to it, a sense of coming full circle.

As I watched my children play, I let my feet tune into my favourite rockpool from all those years ago. None of us are perfect, I thought, as I stood there with my toes in the water. Perfection, I realised, is just a made-up concept, something to make us feel we've failed. Life isn't a flawless storyboard. It's a collection of moments; joyful and painful, messy and beautiful, that weave together to form something far more meaningful than perfection.

We weave them into a story of our lives, and that story, if we tend to it with devotion and rebellion, becomes myth. Not the kind of myth that hides the truth, but the kind that carries truth across time. Our small habits, our mistakes, our joys; they all become threads that future generations may not even know they are holding, yet still feel in their hands.

As I stood listening to the incoming tide now beginning to lap around my feet, I felt that I needed to forgive myself. It was a thought I had resisted for so long. I had carried shame, not just for things I had done, but for things I had failed to do. I had been ungrounded, trying to claim things that weren't mine to begin with. I had taken on roles that weren't truly for me, trying to fit into molds created by others. I had been many facets of myself and played all the roles in all the ways, yet somehow never fully everything at once; and in doing so, I had lost not only my voice but sight of who I truly was as a whole.

It wasn't too late, because it is never too late, I told myself. I had learnt to stop blaming myself and others. I had spent years chasing validation in places that didn't serve me, collecting things — promotions, achievements; things that ultimately felt hollow. I could look at those attempts now and smile. I had learnt so much, and the lessons were valuable.

Old parts of me had died and been reborn, remembered and rewoven and yet the story of me remained. The parts of me I thought it was best we forget; those bitchy parts and those parts that are a little rough around the edges? They could co-exist and make huge changes in the world, in my world, if I used my voice.

I sat back and felt my body. The truth was that I was exhausted — not just from my own actions, but from carrying my story. Everyone has a story, I thought, and for too long I had kept mine hidden, tucked away in the corners of my mind and my body. But stories have to be released; they don't stay silent forever, because stories deserve to be heard in one form or another.

I felt a quiet peace wash over me. As I sat there, tears silently falling, I called back every part of myself that had been lost or hidden away. My teenage confidence, shattered by the harsh judgments of others. My voice, never quite good enough for the world's standards of "stardom" and yet, teenage me knew there were constellations in the power of my voice. My wisdom, once dismissed, and every fragment of me that I had shoved into that prison cell of shame, errors and wrong turns. I called it back.

Something within me clicked into alignment. I felt the energy of those forgotten pieces flood back as if I had been made whole again and I knew that, for the first time in a long while, I was free.

This moment — with the Sun setting and the wind against my skin — felt like a threshold. I had crossed it, and as I stood there with my toes back in my flip-flops, I realised that there are some moments you can never fully explain to anyone. They are felt in the marrow of your bones and the pulse of your heartbeat. They are yours and yours alone to be whispered rather than sang in a song or printed on page.

I knew this feeling needed to be shared somehow. I wondered if I could hand it over to my selkie sisters and perhaps the lineage of the mermaids would carry it off for me, but my gut confirmed this wasn't a match. But as I stood on the slope of the beach and asked out loud, "What do I do with the story of mine now?" Out of nowhere, the wind seemed to howl as if in confirmation that my question had been received.

In the car the next day, as we made our way back up north, we played the manifesting game. My husband asked how I would spend my millions and I let myself dream. We play this all the time on long journeys, I lead him through all the people we would give money to, how we would tell them and the home we would buy in the town that has always felt like home.

He talks about fast cars and trips to far-off places we have seen in documentaries and, by the end of it, I am crying; overwhelmed by the possibility of it all with joy and emotional exhaustion mixed together. This time, we talked about moving to Cornwall when the children were older; "When the timing is right, maybe in two years." We stopped for coffee and a much-needed 'panic pee.'

Halfway home, I wrote the following in my journal, letting the pen lead with no thought or concern for what would come through:

Your soul was born into the great weave of time, drawn forth from mystery into light. You, child, like all, arrived not knowing the path ahead, yet already carrying the seeds within of countless stories to come. Through trials and triumphs, losses and loves, the world shaped you, and you will shape the world in turn. It is time to reframe the possibility of what it means to be human.

You left the safety of the known, stepping into the wilderness of choice and consequence. There were moments of fire — passion, pain, transformation. There were nights of shadow doubt, despair and loneliness, and yet the pull of the luminous thread called you forward.

Guides appeared, some in fleeting whispers, others in great stormful situations. Masks were worn and shed. Names were given and outgrown. Now, at this threshold, your story is still unfolding. What was once sought may no longer be the true prize. What was once feared may now be an ally. The past does not chain you — it feeds the forge of what comes next.

For the story is not over. The most ancient still watch from above and below. The heart still beats. The myth, still alive, asks only this: "What now, weaver? Will you put your story on the page as promised? Will you walk to the edge of magic with us?"

I closed my eyes, tears slipping down my cheeks, and whispered softly, "Lead the way, I trust you." My head was slowly nodding before my mind had a chance to let this idea fully settle within me. "And so it is agreed," someone whispered over my shoulder, and that very same voice has continued to guide me through these pages of doubt and self-discovery right up until today.

I shoved my journal back into the glovebox and turned up the radio, a familiar song filling the space around us.

Within twenty minutes of unpacking at home, we received notice on our house of seven years. I stumbled back through the garden and said to my husband, "It's not two years, it's two months."

I sat on the swing chair in our garden, surrounded by suitcases that seemed a little pointless to unpack – letting the fear move through me, aware it was here to stay for at least the next few months. As the last of the Sun faded, I whispered a quiet thank you to the land, to my journey, to all the parts of me I had called back. There was no other place in the world where I could have written this book, the land knew that.

How we would get to Cornwall, I had no idea. But at this moment, I trusted the unfolding of my little family's story. I trusted that everything would align as it was meant to and that together we could push ourselves to the magickal edge as I had agreed.

The journey was far from over, but I was ready to keep walking; to keep weaving.

And the myth — my myth — was only just beginning.

Letter to self —

You are going to write a book!!

It's going to be so much fun, but it's also going to be hard work. Be consistent, chip away at it. You'll probably cry a lot, you will want to give up, but you must put it all on the page, out of your body and mind and onto paper, only then can you move forward. I am so bloody proud of you.

But remember to be proud of yourself Charlie, you might not believe it counts, but it does.

Being proud of yourself is stronger than anyone else's praise.

Your voice is the mission. Never forget that and keep moving forward because the past has nothing new for you.

Oceans of love Cxx

THE VOICES THAT SHAPE US

Now that you've walked this road with me; through the silence, the performance, the rebellion and the reclamation, I want to return to the idea of three voices. Not because I have mastered it perfectly or to tie it all in a pretty pink bow, but because I've lived it I can now speak of it fully. Throughout this journey, I've come to see that so much of my — and our — struggle is to belong, to be seen and to be at peace. And that comes down to how we relate to three particular voices.

We each carry these three voices with us, whether we're aware of them or not. They speak into our days, our decisions, and our dreams. But if we don't learn to distinguish them, they blur into a hum of confusion that leaves us wondering, "is this really me?"

The first time I became aware of these voices, I didn't have names for them. I just knew that part of me was always speaking, whispering, warning, questioning. Another part tried to put those whispers into words — sometimes bravely, sometimes not at all. Then there was the noise — everyone else's voices; the loud, unrelenting noise of shoulds, musts, you're too much, you're not enough.

The Inner Voice — The one that knows before you know. The one you feel in your gut, your bones and your breath. This voice is not loud, but steady; it's the whisper beneath the noise. It doesn't demand you give you a clear answer as to why it is leading you in a particular direction, it never stops showing up day after day, just hoping you'll listen to your inner inner support system. This is your compass, and though it's not always comfortable, it's always honest. And when you stop long enough to listen, you remember who you are.

Our inner voices have subtle ways of getting our attention, rarely speaks in complete sentences, and yet it knows things before we do. Sometimes it's a nudge, a tightening in the chest, a sudden calm, or a phrase that repeats in your mind for days until you finally stop to listen. It lives deeper than thought in the body and in the spirit. Some call it intuition, others call it God, or the higher self. I don't argue with any of those, I just know this: my inner voice is the truest thing I have.

But for most of my life, I didn't trust it. I trusted the reason, logic, evidence and audience feedback. And mostly, I trusted what other people thought of me. I mistook my fear for wisdom and my overthinking for insight. But the inner voice doesn't beg to be trusted, it just waits.

It wasn't until my life started feeling like someone else's that I went inward; not to escape, but to return. I needed to turn the volume down on everything else to be able to hear that whisper of the voice I was once ungrounded, and yet very comfortable with. What I found was my current true voice, because like most things in life, nothing ever stays the same.

The Outer Voice — The one the world hears. The one that speaks truth, or hides it.
This voice is how we show up, how we say *yes* and how we say *no*. It's our story in motion. For so long, I didn't know how to use this voice; I either over-explained or went silent. But with time, I learned that I didn't need to sound perfect, I just needed to sound *true*. Because truth is a vibe you and the person you share with can feel.

Once you start hearing your inner voice, the next step is learning how to speak it. The part of you that says, "This is who I am, this is what I need, this is what I love, this is what I will no longer tolerate."

This voice took me years to find. I was fluent in people-pleasing, trained in silence, and skilled at saying just enough to control a room and stay safe. A true voice though? That required something else. It required truth, vulnerability, risk, and that truth gave me much more than safety; it gave me freedom.

The outer voice is what bridges your inner world with the outer one. It's not just speaking, it's expressing. Your outer voice is your *courage in motion*. But here's the thing: it doesn't always sound pretty. It may shake, it may say the wrong thing, it may contradict what others expect, but it's yours. And, once it is only yours, it begins to evolve.

The more I spoke from my truth, the clearer it became; not always easier, but clearer. Finding your outer voice doesn't mean shouting – there is too much of this already. Finding this part of your voice means showing up as your whole self and that, I've learned, is one of the most radical things you can do in today's world.

The Voice of the World – The loudest. The most persistent. It says: "Be like them. Do it right. Stay small. Speak up. Not like that." It tells you who to be before you've had a chance to ask yourself who you *want* to be. Sometimes it's wise; often it's simply noise. The world's voice is always there, but we choose how much power we give it.

The world has a voice too. It has many, actually. They come from your culture, your family, your history; from the media, religion, teachers, friends, strangers; even from centuries of collective human insecurity. The voice of the world tells you what success looks like, what beauty should be, how much is enough and what kind of life is worth living.

Sometimes these voices are helpful. They teach, they warn and they reflect where we've come from. But more often, they blur your own voice; they hijack your thoughts until you forget what you even wanted in the first place. I've lived whole seasons of my life under the weight of the world's voice; shaping myself to fit into spaces that weren't mine and performing a life that felt impressive, but not true. It's exhausting.

The world will always have something to say, but we don't have to internalise all of it as our own. Learning which voices to let in and which to let pass is spiritual discernment in practice and it changes everything. I curse myself that I listened to the world for too long, but if I hadn't then I don't suppose this book would have come to exist.

Harmony: The True Voice Emerges

So here's what I've come to believe: When your inner voice is clear, your outer voice is aligned and the world's voice is filtered wisely, you begin to live from your true voice. Not just the one you speak, but the one you live.

That's the voice that doesn't need to shout to be heard; the one that moves through the world with grounded confidence, living by example and not to convince anyone else but to live the life that is true to you.

This journey of listening, refining, and expressing is sacred. It is slow and it is ongoing, but it is the journey of becoming. I'm not entirely sure we will ever know what it is we are fully becoming either; it's a sort of endless peeling back of layers and a never-ending spiral of evolution. We will make 'mistakes', over-explain, sparkle sentences with F-ombs when we don't have a more elegant word on the tip of our tongue; but this is the joy and the turmoil found in the journey of the human voice.

The True Voice: When your inner voice is heard, your outer voice is aligned, and the world's voice is filtered with wisdom, something beautiful happens. You begin to live in your true voice — not just the one you speak, but the one you *embody*.

Reminder — The persistence of Shame

Shame is something we never fully outgrow as human beings. We often hear people claim they feel no shame, but more often than not that's just bravado. When the world is quiet and we're alone with ourselves, if we dig deep enough, we can all find something that stirs a sense of shame. (For the record, I don't recommend doing this at two in the morning — nothing good comes from late-night overthinking.)

At its core, shame is fear in disguise. Fear blocks us from speaking in our true voice, and shame is its favorite mask. I've felt shame about so many things in different stages of my life: not being able to drive, having a big nose, choosing a different educational path for my children, even the balance in my bank account.

But here's what I've learned: when shame is spoken aloud, it begins to dissolve. The truth may be uncomfortable, but once we face it and name it, it loses its grip. I've tried countless ways to "fix" myself — many of which I haven't even touched on here — but the turning point wasn't found in changing who I was. It came from accepting myself as I am in every moment.

THE WHISPERS OF THE NEXT CHAPTER

Always go a little further into the water than you feel you're capable of being in. Go a little bit out of your depth. And when you don't feel that your feet are quite touching the bottom, you're just about in the right place to do something exciting.

— David Bowie

Within the first year of moving, not only were we emotionally broken but I physically took a tumble at the half way point of this book. I never quite know when we cross the invisible age barrier from 'falling over' and 'having a fall'. One seems to be something we only say when someone is elderly for some reason. So instead, let's stick with tumble. I tumbled over on a coastal path, and if it wasn't for the hedgerow that stopped me, then I would have tumbled right off the edge and onto the rocks.

The tumble shook me to my core and left me with no choice but to rest indoors for several months, then slowly rebuild my strength. So I wrote this book, all whilst feeling at my most broken physically. My body felt weak and I hated it; up until this point I had no ailments or physical limitations worth noting, but for the first time I could feel a fragility in my humanness both on the page and in my life.

The thoughts went through my head: What if I left everything I wanted to do until it was too late? What if I can't swim alone anymore? What if I wanted to run a marathon?! (Yes, I really did, for a very brief moment of downward spiraling, consider this as a possibility! For the record I don't run for anything, ever.) To many, this may seem like a rather pathetic spiral but honestly, until this point I had been lucky. I felt this huge shame and failure that I hadn't reached all the goals I wanted to reach, that I hadn't written my first book back when I had the idea at the time my children still took afternoon naps.

I looked at my body so differently to how I used to. It wasn't simply a shell that the world only wished was smaller, it was a part of me; every line, every scar and every curve was a story in every sense of the word. Even if she felt somehow old, outdated and broken on the sofa.

Until I was living and sleeping on the sofa with a stack of journals and a notebook, I don't suppose I had realised how bridge-like these years had become. I wasn't a maiden any more, and I most definitely was not in my crone phase of life; I was somewhere in between — in a spot along the journey with no signposts.

The world might constantly tell us we are outdated. To be honest I don't know if I'm a millennial or an elderly millennial; I'm not actually fussed. What I was fussed about was that I hadn't realised, until I was forced to sit in one spot, how forty doesn't really have a place for a lot of the world. It's not glamorous to have wrinkles, or need to wear a size bigger jeans.

I could have sprinted towards the town marked 'menopause' like so many others, yet in true, stubborn wisdom, I sat in the unknown on the sofa with a body I didn't feel was my own or was worthy of taking up as much space as it did. And so I wrote and I wrote. I felt guilty for writing, I woke up in the middle of the night to write, I made notes in the middle of the supermarket of things I wanted to write, and the pages began to unfold.

Nine months had passed and I had hardly left the house, curled up on the yellow bench at my kitchen table. I am so grateful to my family for their patience whilst I healed, reconnected and learnt to trust my body again.

After so many months, I could hear the sea calling me. I kept quiet about it, not sure my body or my mind was ready. Until the evening my husband suggested we visit a cave that I hadn't been to since we moved, and so we set the alarms. The next morning, I took the long route to avoid the dunes on my recovering foot and I slipped between the folds of the Earth as the wind howled its chilling song.

I let my hands explore the damp, dark ripples of the cave wall; its salt crystals gathering under my fingernails, as if my touch of her ancient scales were unlocking codes meant only for me. The only sounds were the drip-drip-drip from the rocks, the roll of the approaching tide, and the laughter of my children on the sand outside.

I listened again for something more and there was the hum in the back of the cave I had been looking for. Feeling it ripple through my body as drops of water pitter-pattered on my forehead from above, I closed my eyes and smiled, imagining the land herself anointing me into the new year and I sang. Then I asked "*Where do we go from here?*"

A deep, gravel-like voice from the back corner replied, "*You become the living myth.*"

Not entirely understanding, I carried those words with me across the cove, my coat pocket full of shells as we headed back towards the car.

The entire journey home, through the valley and woods, I twirled those words in my mind. This voice seemed to fill the space and create room for something new; something lighter. I didn't fully understand the profound unraveling this phrase would have on my life, but I could feel its potency, like a seed in the pit of my stomach. It would continue to grow for months to come. Now, I was determined to hold both what had been and what was

— and is — to come in my hands, and run.

We are the voice of the Living Myth. The stories of this world grow wilder but guess what? So do we. And, for once in my life, I don't think that's a bad thing — as long as we continue to share from a grounded place of love, not an ungrounded place of fear. (We all know what happens when we share from that place.)

We are the lineage of living stories. Even when it feels like we have no roots or clear direction, I've learned that this is often when the story truly begins. New characters, new beliefs, new adventures and, most likely, a few detours and wrong turns. But aren't they the best stories?

We are creating the myths of the future today, and if that doesn't propel us forward to greater things, I don't know what will. For one day, we will all be myths. Perhaps the change begins when we realise that we always have been.

As synchronicity would have it, that next week I found myself returning finally to the water — swimming out to the pontoon of my childhood summer holidays with the very same friend who sat with me in the luggage compartment of the school bus. My ankle grumbling at the now unfamiliar motion of swimming, I persisted further out until I could no longer touch the sea bed.

Floating out towards the luggar we talked about dreams and plans; all the mistakes we thought we had made, boys we had dated and hated. He talked about houses, cars and goals for the future then he asked me what was next? I rolled off a recent pilgrimage with the vicar from the village we grew up in, a day drip to one of my favourite water falls in the spring and some new plans I was putting into motion for our home.

Then I shared how I am not sure the world knows what to do with women at forty. We tell them they need to look younger or we push them to the back of the line because they're not that pretty any more, or that they have nothing useful to contribute now that they have had kids and worked their 'best years' away. Eyes closed as I contemplated everything that led us here I said, "I'm wondering where I fit in mate?" He smiled. "I don't think you came here to fit in at all, Char."

I nodded. "I know but in all honesty I think it's time to let the old me go, and let the new me lead and not quietly either." We both laughed because, as you probably know now, I have been described as a lot of things – quiet was never one of them.

Nothing is for certain but the first thing I know is I will not be going into the next phase of life quietly. Secondly, I have no intention of joining the 'it's all downhill from here crew'; slipping into full on perimenopausal rage with some false hope that its arrival will honour me with a crown of wisdom. That's not for me.

Instead, intend to stay here in this spot between devotion and rebellion, treading water and somehow also tethered to something sacred. I knew that day something new was stirring within me, something with so much to learn, yet also so much to give. The world could push me to the fringes as hard as it wants – "There's nothing more I love than encouraging a rebellion," I thought as I let the water hold me, just as the land had all those years before.

Wisdom is always woven between the days we feel are least important. Where we aren't sure exactly where we belong and where we stand on the threshold of who we were and who we want to be. In that liminal space where two things collide, I won't rush these years. Instead, I intend to float here and see which way the tide takes me; it hasn't failed me so far.

This is a roll call. A rallying cry. An invitation.

I summon you back –
back to the wild tongue you once silenced,
back to the story that drums in your ribs,
back to the truth that was never lost, only waiting.

Call your voice back from the places you left it. From the swallowed words, the bitten tongue, the sentences cut short only to make space for someone else. Call it back from the ashes of doubt, from the cages of should, and must and silence. It is yours. It has always been yours. No more smallness. No more shame. No more smoothing those sharp edges to fit a world too brittle to hold you.

You are the keeper of your verses, the poet of your own becoming and the maker of myths to come.

So speak.
Speak in the language of fire and riverbend,
in the highs of wolf howl and depths of storms song.
Speak like the sky splitting open,
like the ocean remembering her name,
like a prayer no longer asking but demanding.

This is your return.
This is your reckoning.
This is your remembering.

Tell them now. Tell them whole. Tell them like only you can.

We have and always will be the story tellers of not only the future we want but the future we deserve. For ourselves and for humanity. Call it back, sing it back, write it back for today and all the days that follow.

On the silent wings of the barn owl know your voice will be received in all the ways it is meant to.

RECLAIMING YOUR VOICE

Writing this book has been one of the most amazing and heartbreaking journeys of my life. A collision of all the things. Something I have come to realise is that the most beautiful things are created in those spaces where two or more emotions meet. It has been as transformative as it has been challenging; an experience that brought me face-to-face with my own raw truths and the spaces within me that needed healing.

Above all, it has been a gift, like a key unlocking a door to something I had always known but never fully embraced. The words poured onto the page effortlessly, as if they were meant to be released. I know my poisons and my dosage now. I've sat in the dirt of my actions, feeling the cold, wet heaviness beneath my fingers, but I'm no longer just sitting there. Now, I'm determined to hold both what has been and what is yet to come, and I'm ready to run with them.

For as long as I can remember, spirit has whispered to me, "Your voice is the mission." Over time, that message has morphed and resurfaced in various ways, but its core has remained the same. Each of us has a voice that deserves to be heard, because without our voices, there are no stories, no myths and no legends remembered.

As a woman, I know this truth all too well. We have been silenced for centuries, for our voices are the gateway to change. They unlock our hearts and our wombs, bringing forth new possibilities. Society has tried to teach us to use our sexuality as power, but the truth is, there's a much simpler and less manipulative way: we use our voice. We open up communication channels in our homes, in our hearts, and we share how we feel; we speak out against what we see, what needs to change. But doing so is often harder than it seems.

I knew this even as a teenager sitting in the library or History class. Even as stubborn as I was, I found myself reweaving lost melodies from the past that I couldn't begin to see the power of at the time.

Shame is always going to be there. I've felt shame for the things I've done in my life, shame for the things I've only thought about, and shame for those I have yet to do. Shame isn't going anywhere; that doesn't mean we rewrite our lives in hopes to make them more palatable, or that we stop telling stories entirely.

Using our voices opens doors, not just for us but for those around us. It removes generational fences and creates a path for those who will follow. So let's tell tales. Let's speak loudly – not over others, but so our voices can be heard. Let us claw back the parts of our voice that were taken and used for someone else's agenda.

There is one thing I do know for sure: Our voices are the first reclamation of power we must take back.

There was a time when human voices were pure; raw, unfiltered, and deeply connected to the Earth. Even with all our emotions, we spoke freely, unburdened by fear. Our words would dance between realms. But somewhere along the way, we learned to quiet those voices. The whispers of self-doubt, the weight of expectations, and the pressure to be perfect dulled the sound we once carried so effortlessly.

We were taught that silence was safer; that our words were either too much or too little. We were told that softness was a virtue, but strength had to be loud — just not too loud.

So we fell into the shadows of our own stories, as if staying quiet would protect us from the world that seemed determined to make us shrink. And in doing so, we abandoned parts of ourselves that desperately needed to be heard.

Humanity has worn a mask for too long. We've forgotten what it feels like to speak from the deepest parts of ourselves. We adapted and conformed, but the truth is that no mask can capture the essence of who we truly are.

This journey is about reclaiming our voices — not only as an act of defiance, but of remembrance. We are unlearning the stories that told us to be small and stepping back into the narrative we've always been meant to write. It's time to speak not only the words we've held inside but the truth buried beneath them. Our voices, once silent, now rise in the fullness of who we've always been.

Final Heart Thread — Your voice is the mission

When I started writing this book, it was never meant to be a "how-to" guide. In fact, for much of it, we could probably call it more of a "how not-to" guide; an invitation to return to our own voices, despite the noise of the world and the pressure of society. But as I near the end, I want to leave you with something to carry forward, because sometimes, we need things spelled out for us.

There are many lessons I've learned, some of which I hope are helpful to you. But if you take away nothing else, remember this: Your story matters. The voices in your head, the emotional currents that run through your body — they matter. That's why we're here.

So what is a story? A story is simply words shared, they don't have to be written on a page. Please share them. Speak openly and honestly, more often. You don't need to write a book, but there are countless ways to share your story beyond the methods we're often shown; journal, write poetry, speak to the land, sing songs, tell tales.

We've all been silenced — especially women. If there's one thing writing this book has taught me, it's that we need more communication channels that bypass social media and the world's current idea of entertainment.

When we look through history, we see how many of our beliefs, our fears, and society's quiet rules are woven into the stories we share. Women who tell stories are powerful. They aren't shrouded in shame, nor diminished by being told they are "just mothers" and not yet "wise women."

Throughout every phase of our lives, we're told we aren't enough. But by sharing our stories in those very moments, we become more than we've ever been told. We become united and ignited.

I pulled many threads for this book from years of journals, but even then, it wasn't enough. I wished, over and over, that I had shared the stories as they came. How much I would've learned, how much I would've grown, and how much lighter and freer I would have felt — not just as a woman, but as a human.

The voice of living myth calls us to share; share when we're in the thick of it, share when we've just had that big realisation. It's how we're seen, how we're heard, and how we become closer to each other.

We've talked about how, through fear of shame, we hold our tongues when given space to share. But what I've learned is this: we might fear the shame, but what those who keep us quiet fear is the power that comes from sharing.

So please, continue to tell your tales. Whether it's to a friend, a family member, or a professional; just share. As long as you share, my work here is done.

Revisiting these chapters of my life has been a rollercoaster, and if you consider that I don't even like crossing over a humpback bridge, it's a miracle I made it this far. It would be a lie to say I didn't want to give up several times throughout this journey.

But when we commit to sharing from a place of devotion, a shift happens. We no longer begin to look at our stories through a lens of shame or as if they were a tragedy, we see them as fulfilment or a rite of passage; a gateway of who we are today.

Have you ever met a woman who simply shows up? No doubts, no hesitation, perhaps she waits to speak last, or perhaps she speaks slightly more quietly than needed so the men around the table have to lean in to hear her.

Others speak first, knowing women have been waiting for far too long. There is no wrong or right way, there simply is an opening and an allowing to flow. This is what we must do. In all the places and spaces. Not tomorrow, not next week or when we are physically taking up less room in our jeans. Now.

If we wait until we know it all, or for the perfect moment, we should know those things rarely happen. Yet we have this misconception that we have a final destination to reach; a place of divine knowing, of completeness; a conclusion with many names. But I don't believe there's an end — to life, to lessons, or to learning. I believe it's all a spiral; a labyrinth of rebirth and rediscovery. So with that in mind there is never a perfect or imperfect time to share.

Share your dreams, your hopes, your feelings, your ideas and your fears. Share them in safe spaces and wild spaces. Let them dance along your vocal cords, up and out into the world. That's the invitation of this book. Not just to find your voice, but to live it. Fully. Freely. Faithfully.

Writing this book taught me that we're taught to hate our wild, feral edges. The truth is, our wholeness begins when we expand our hearts around all the 'broken; parts of us. Some call them sins, mistakes, or errors in judgment. But when we embrace them as part of our lives — and of our souls — we learn to love ourselves and our stories again. This was the ultimate truth I had swallowed over and over again.

Our stories are the foundations we build upon, so let's make them solid ones; ones of truth that we chose to keep. I didn't begin this journey of acceptance until I was in my late thirties. Don't wait that long.

Someone once told me that wisdom isn't something you pray for—it's something you earn. Sometimes it comes with scars. Other times, it hides between the pages of very old, "accidentally" lost books, or in the quiet corners of forgotten art. For me, it came through the writing of this book, and I hope that a little of that wisdom drifts from the page and settles gently in your heart.

Revisiting my life so far reminded me that I can be both wrong and right, that I can speak and also hold silence to truly listen. We can all be more than one thing at a time: fierce and tender, devoted and rebellious.

Oceans of love, Cx

My deepest gratitude

The art of storytelling requires a person to remain in a state of extreme vulnerability for long periods of time — we have to feel everything to be able to share it so deeply.

I would be foolish to think I could have done this work without people in my life who love me and who have put me back together when I felt the weight of this task. Without you all, I would never be able to click the publish button.

To my husband — Thank you for encouraging me to remain wild. With you I learned what it is to be truly seen, safe, and supported. This is a gift I can never find enough words to express my gratitude for. Simply know you are forever the anchor to my existence. xx

To my world — Boo Bear & Hero Bear, thank you for always showing up as your truest selves and encouraging me to do the same. Being your mother is the greatest honour and lesson I will ever have in any lifetime. I am eternally in awe of each of you. If I had one wish it would be that you will always know the immense light you bring into the world. xx

Kerry W — I often wonder what the world needs more of, and then I remember you and the love you share with everyone you meet. Thank you for including me in that circle. To the Wiltshire girls — You chose one of the best families to be born into and a lineage of women who are strong, brave, and incredibly kind. Never forget that. Love Beach Charlie

Ceryn — Without your encouragement, patience, and wisdom, I might never have reached this day of publishing. Thank you for the kindness you share so generously with the world and for the light you've brought to my journey. I will always be grateful for the path that led me to you.

Yolandi – Thank you for your laughter and acceptance, you gave us shelter during the hardest time of our life and for this alone I will always have your back even during your most crazy of ideas. But above all thank you for bringing so much FAAFO energy into my life even when I didn't think I needed it.

My dearest friends – Louis, Adele, Emma, Jo, Em & Becky,– Once upon a time I sat under the weeping willow of my childhood playing field and put out a call for each of you. The universe did not disappoint, and I appreciate you all in your own magickal ways. I love you all.

To Cornwall herself, my eternal home – You called me back. Deep down, I always knew you would. The eight-year-old girl within me is regularly stunned by your wild beauty and wicked humour. Forever honoured to do this work with you and to call this land my home.

To my spirit kin and the ancestors who walk beside me every day – "Thank you" never quite feels like enough, but I hope you can feel how deeply I adore you.

And finally, to the people I have yet to meet on my path: I will place a seat at my table in anticipation of your arrival. Until the day we meet, simply know that I love you already.

www.ingramcontent.com/pod-product-compliance
Ingram Content Group UK Ltd.
Pitfield, Milton Keynes, MK11 3LW, UK
UKHW020907081225
9431UKWH00048B/1058

9 781036 964375